Library of
Davidson College

THE UNFINISHED AGENDA

MEMBERS OF THE ENVIRONMENTAL AGENDA TASK FORCE

Gerald O. Barney
Rockefeller Brothers Fund

John H. Adams
Natural Resources Defense Council

David R. Brower
Friends of the Earth

George D. Davis
The Wilderness Society

Robert T. Dennis
Zero Population Growth

Thomas L. Kimball
National Wildlife Federation

Ian C. T. Nisbet
Massachusetts Audubon Society

G. Jon Roush
The Nature Conservancy

Arlie Schardt
Environmental Defense Fund

Maitland S. Sharpe
Izaak Walton League of America

Anthony Wayne Smith
National Parks and Conservation Association

Elvis J. Stahr
National Audubon Society

Paul Swatek
Sierra Club

THE CITIZEN'S POLICY GUIDE TO ENVIRONMENTAL ISSUES

THE UNFINISHED AGENDA

A Task Force Report Sponsored by the Rockefeller Brothers Fund

Edited by Gerald O. Barney

THOMAS Y. CROWELL COMPANY
Established 1834 • New York

Copyright © 1977 by the Rockefeller Brothers Fund
All rights reserved. Except for use in a review, the reproduction or utilization of this work in any form or by any electronic, mechanical, or other means, now known or hereafter invented, including xerography, photocopying, and recording, and in any information storage and retrieval system is forbidden without the written permission of the publisher. Published simultaneously in Canada by Fitzhenry & Whiteside Limited, Toronto.

Manufactured in the United States of America

Library of Congress Cataloging in Publication Data

Main entry under title:
The Unfinished agenda.

Includes bibliographical references and index.
1. Environmental policy—United States.
I. Barney, Gerald O. II. Rockefeller Brothers Fund.
HC110.E5U5   301.31'0973   76-30486
ISBN 0-690-01481-3
ISBN 0-690-01482-1 (pbk.)

1 3 5 7 9 10 8 6 4 2

Contents

Preface/1

Acknowledgments/7

Editor's Note/9

Introduction: The Call to Action/11

1. POPULATION: HOW MANY IS TOO MANY?/23

Population Growth/23

A Fourfold Program/28

2. FOOD AND AGRICULTURE/34

International Population Control/38

Redistribution of Food Supplies/39

Increasing Agricultural Production/42

The Chemical Fertilizer Problem/47

3. The Energy Economy/50

The Current Dilemma/51

The Nuclear Controversy/53

The Energy Blueprint/59

The Policy Challenge/64

4. Natural Resources: Will They Last?/69

The Advantages of Recycling/71

The Advantages of Re-use/74

The Future of Mineral Supplies and Other Materials/74

Water: A Special Resource Problem/77

5. Water and Air Pollution/81

Air and Water Pollution Regulation/81

Sludge/90

6. The Hazards of Toxic Substances/92

Effective Regulation: Still a Possibility?/94

The Toxic Substances Control Act/96

Financial Priorities/96

7. Spaceship Earth: The Life-Support System/99

Public Lands in the United States/100

Private Land-Use Regulation/115

The U.S. Role in Protecting the Global Ecosystem/118

A Land Ethic/121

8. THE NEW BIOLOGICAL THREAT/123

The Hazards of Recombinant DNA Research/124

Protection for Humanity and the Environment/127

9. SOCIETY AND DECISION-MAKING/132

National Planning/133

Technology Control/139

A Priority: Organizing the Federal Agencies/142

Industry as the Decision-Maker/144

Educating the Public/151

10. A QUESTION OF VALUES/155

Appendix: The Environmental Movement/161

Notes/167

Index/179

Preface

"POLLUTION ISN'T HURTING ME personally, so what's the fuss about? Isn't a little pollution just the price we have to pay for progress? Is it all that bad? We can't return the countryside to the way it was before the first Kleenex was dropped, so what do environmentalists want, anyway?"

These and similar questions have been asked by many people like you and me wishing that there were simple answers. But whom does one ask? Who are the so-called environmentalists? We have all met a few, but since they occasionally seem to have difficulty agreeing, whom is one to believe? They appear to come from very diverse backgrounds, yet they do share a common passion of caring about life on this planet.

The Environmental Agenda Project* was an effort to find out what environmentalists in fact want; in the course of this project it became clear that there exist in this country a very large number of environmentalists concerned

---

*This project was funded by the Rockefeller Brothers Fund, and a member of the Fund's staff, Gerald O. Barney, served a catalytic function by assisting the participants in drawing the material together and in editing this report.

with a broad range of issues. The wave of environmental concern has been growing for decades, to the point where environmental awareness is now part of the conscious social concerns of virtually everyone. No one now can afford to be indifferent to the massive contamination of a local river by cancer-inducing chemicals or to the large-scale human activities that are altering critical properties of the earth's entire atmosphere. Another indication of the numbers of citizens concerned about the environment is the election-day effectiveness of Environmental Action's list of the "Dirty Dozen" congressmen and the League of Conservation Voters' "Voters' Guide."

The Environmental Agenda Project was an effort to enlist the constructive thinking of the nation's most knowledgeable and professional environmental leaders. These experts came from a growing number of lawyers, scientists, engineers, journalists, and other professionals who have decided to devote their lives to environmental work. Sixty-three of these new leaders pooled their considerable expertise, in the first place, to identify and describe what they regarded as the most critical issues this nation must face up to during the next decade, and secondly to recommend what explicit actions might be taken over the next several years, if not to solve these problems, then at least to take steps in the right direction. Since the problems are complex and long-term, it would be a serious mistake for anyone to think that there are quick or easy solutions.

As so many people contributed to the project, it is important to understand how the report was prepared. Recognizing the progress on environmental problems already made, the project's members concentrated on the specific and as yet unfulfilled needs—The Unfinished Agenda.

As a start for the agenda, 25 participants provided a total of 140 short assessments of what they regarded as the

Preface

key problems to be faced. This initial list of 140 ideas went to all the participants, who were then asked to identify the most significant problems and to add others that might come to mind. Short papers on the topics that thus emerged as "most important" were prepared and integrated into an initial draft report which again was shared with all of the participants. The Task Force members, one each from the twelve largest direct-membership environmental organizations, then met in New York for an all-day review of the draft. The draft report was subsequently rewritten based on the recommendations of the Task Force and on numerous suggestions and comments from the other participants.

This document, therefore, is a consensus document. It expresses ideas that, in the collective thinking of the participating environmental leaders, represent the most important problems of the coming decade. Although the participants were in substantial agreement on the content of the report, individuals may have had reservations on one or more specific points. Also, since the participants spoke as individuals rather than as representatives of their respective organizations, the ideas expressed here have not been endorsed by any organization, including the Rockefeller Brothers Fund. The report is put forward simply as a consensus statement of what the participating environmental leaders regard as the Unfinished Agenda.

In addition to those members of the Task Force whose names appear at the beginning of this book, the following people participated in the project (affiliations are noted for identification purposes only):

James Aldrich, Alliance for Environmental Education; Frederick Anderson, Environmental Law Institute; James Benson, Energy Research & Development Administration; Lester R. Brown, Worldwatch Institute; Robert Cahn, The Conservation Foundation; Chester L. Cooper, Institute for Energy Analysis of Oak Ridge, Tennessee;

Herman Daly, Louisiana State University; J. Clarence Davies III, The Conservation Foundation; Henry Diamond, Citizens Advisory Committee on Environmental Quality; Dennis Drabelle, Department of the Interior; Daniel Ford, Union of Concerned Scientists; Jay W. Forrester, Massachusetts Institute of Technology; Allen Green, Garden Way Associates; Willis Harman, Center for the Study of Social Policy, Stanford University; Peter Harnick, Environmental Action; Hazel Henderson, Princeton Center for Alternative Futures, Inc.; Joseph Highland, Environmental Defense Fund; Charles Hitch, Resources for the Future; John Holdren, Energy & Resources Program, University of California, Berkeley; John Humke, The Nature Conservancy; Clifford Humphrey, Ecology Action Educational Institute; T. Destry Jarvis, National Parks and Conservation Association; Huey D. Johnson, Trust for Public Land; Dorothy Kuper, League of Women Voters; George Lamb, American Conservation Association; Thomas A. Lawand, Institut de Recherches Brace; Thomas V. Long, Resource Analysis Group, University of Chicago; Amory B. Lovins, Friends of the Earth; Alice Tepper Marlin, Council on Economic Priorities; Allan McGowan, Scientists' Institute for Public Information; John and Magda McHale, Center for Integrated Studies, State University of New York; George McRobie, Intermediate Technology Development Institute; Dennis Meadows, Club of Rome and Dartmouth College; Donella Meadows, Dartmouth College; James Moorman, Sierra Club Legal Defense Fund; Al Moran, Planned Parenthood; David Pimentel, Department of Entomology, Cornell University; William K. Reilly, The Conservation Foundation; Laurance Rockefeller, Natural Resources Defense Council; Charles Ryan, Massachusetts Institute of Technology; Robert Stein, International Institute for Environment and Development; Larry Stevens, Citizens Advisory Committee on Environmental Quality;

Robert Stecker, A. T. & T. Long Lines Division; Thomas Stoel, Natural Resources Defense Council; John Todd, New Alchemy Institute; Nancy Todd, New Alchemy Institute; Joanna Underwood, INFORM; Carroll Wilson, Massachusetts Institute of Technology; George Zeidenstein, The Population Council.

Copies of the draft materials were also sent to the following people: Al Alm, Environmental Protection Agency; Russell Beaton, Economics Department, Willamette University; Thomas Bender, RAIN; Murray Bookchin, Institute for Social Ecology; Joseph Browder, Environmental Policy Center; Barry Commoner, Center for the Biology of Natural Systems, Washington University; Marion Edey, League of Conservation Voters; Harold Green, George Washington University; Richard Hough, National Defense University; Robert Heilbroner, New School for Social Research; Steven Jellinek, Council on Environmental Quality; Gordon McDonald, Center for Environmental Studies, Dartmouth College; John Milton, Threshold; Ralph Nader, Center for the Study of Responsive Law; Emma Rothschild, writer; William Ruckelshaus, Ruckelshaus, Beveridge, Fairbanks & Diamond; Edward Wenk, Jr., University of Washington; Robert H. Williams, Center for Environmental Studies, Princeton University.

Acknowledgments

THE FOLLOWING PEOPLE (whose affiliations are noted where necessary for identification) contributed papers on specific issues for inclusion in the report: Gerald O. Barney; Judith Lee Brown, Rockefeller Brothers Fund; Lester R. Brown, Worldwatch Institute; Robert Chipley, The Nature Conservancy; Herman Daly, Louisiana State University; J. Clarence Davies III, The Conservation Foundation; Daniel Ford, Union of Concerned Scientists; Jay W. Forrester, Massachusetts Institute of Technology; Joseph Highland, Environmental Defense Fund; Clifford Humphrey, Ecology Action Educational Institute; T. Destry Jarvis, National Parks and Conservation Association; Thomas V. Long, University of Chicago; Amory Lovins, Friends of the Earth; Donella Meadows, Dartmouth College; Ian C. T. Nisbet, Massachusetts Audubon Society; David Pimentel, Cornell University; Patricia Rambach, Sierra Club; William K. Reilly, The Conservation Foundation; Katharine Smith, Rockefeller Brothers Fund; Thomas Stoel, Natural Resources Defense Council; Nicholas Wade, *Science* Magazine.

Several people contributed to the editing and preparation of the report. Among these, Katharine Smith played an especially important role in keeping things moving along smoothly on a tight schedule. Donella Meadows, Ian Nisbet, Laurance Rockefeller (Natural Resources Defense Council), Arlie Schardt, Joseph Highland, and George Davis all assisted in rewriting sections of the report. Editorial assistance was provided by Alison Bond, Eleanor Sypher, Pamela Jones, Albert Farnsworth, Anthony Wolff, Katharine Smith, and Judith Brown. Patricia Badum and Katharine Smith managed the actual preparation of the drafts.

Editor's Note

THE UNFINISHED AGENDA is organized in three sections, unequal in length but not in significance. The introductory section provides a summary of the basic recommendations of the Unfinished Agenda. Since these recommendations are of prime importance, and are urgent in their appeal, they precede the main chapters dealing with specific aspects of the problem rather than follow in the more usual concluding form. One overall recommendation is that the individual recommendations be taken up in a way that does not neglect either the long-term or the short-term dimensions of the problem.

Chapters 1 through 8 discuss in greater detail the visible and specific aspects of the environmental problem—the human population and the physical resources necessary for the sustenance and satisfaction of that population: land, food, energy, resources, water, air, and the biologic life-support system of other living species that provides life, beauty, and pleasure.

Chapter 9 takes up some of the difficulties underlying society's decisions that have contributed to these physical problems. Two major decision centers of society—government and industry—are discussed in terms of their influence, both institutional and educational, on the decisions, actions, and values of individuals. The final chapter focuses on individual values and their implications for the environment.

G.O.B.

Introduction: The Call to Action

THE ENVIRONMENT IS a complex mixture of factors which interact constantly with each other: People need food; raising food requires energy; energy production utilizes materials from the earth's crust; the extraction of these materials demands energy; and all of these activities depend upon the labor and ingenuity of people, who need food. Thus when any single factor in the environment is altered, either intentionally or accidentally, the repercussions are felt throughout the entire system. The human population, an integral component of the ecosystem, influences and ultimately is affected by these alterations; the environmental actions that this country decides to take will affect everyone. Because ill-considered changes that may have irreversible consequences threaten our welfare, immediate action on some issues is critical.

POPULATION

If the current annual population growth continues, the world population, which is now about 4 billion, will reach 8 billion soon after the year 2000. Most of the number added will be poor families in poor nations with insufficient food supplies. On a global scale therefore it is recommended that:

- **Continuation and increased funding of family planning programs, research into fertility control methods, and training of paramedical personnel in recipient nations be provided** to administer and follow up on simple techniques of contraception, abortion, and sterilization.
- **Special emphasis be given to foreign-aid measures that have an indirect negative effect on fertility, such as female education, female employment, or social security programs.**

A population policy for the U.S. should aim for two interrelated goals: to increase the quality of life experienced by the population and to stabilize the population size. To this end, several basic goals are recommended:

- **Establish a national goal of population stabilization or gradual population decrease, with the small family as a desirable and socially responsible ideal.**
- **Increase support for established family planning organizations and provide aid for clinics that offer contraceptives, pregnancy testing, abortion, and sterilization.**
- **Establish sex and family education programs, especially for pre-teens and teenagers.**
- **Give positive publicity to women in positions of responsibility and authority and to the creative possibilities open to those with small families.**
- **Remove taxation discriminations against single people and childless couples and eliminate additional tax benefits for those with three or more children.**
- **Make day-care facilities, paternity and maternity leaves, flexible work schedules and other such measures available to permit coordination of parenthood duties with other career duties.**
- **Provide education for stable marriage and responsible parenthood and encourage public education in the basics of demography.**

Introduction

- **Gradually reduce and stabilize quotas for legal immigration and take steps to encourage economic development in countries which are significant sources of illegal aliens, to remove the root causes of immigration.**
- **Congress should adopt a policy statement on immigration which relates immigration to national population, resources, employment, and education policies.**

FOOD AND AGRICULTURE

During the 1950s and 60s, the world agriculture system produced more food than could be sold; during the early 70s the situation changed markedly. World demand for food outstripped the capacity of farmers and fishermen to produce. At its lowest point, the world carry-over stores of grain were capable of meeting less than one month's demand.

In some parts of the world, such as Bangladesh, food shortages are severe enough to interfere with population growth by raising death rates, at least in years of bad weather. In the Sahel, Ethiopia, Nepal, and the Andean area of South America, explosive population rates could actually undermine and destroy major food-producing systems, doing enormous environmental damage in the process.

Three approaches are possible for the world food problem: increase food production, redistribute more effectively the food that is already grown, or stabilize world population growth. U.S. policy currently emphasizes the first of these, through agricultural research, economic aid and agricultural assistance, and export of surplus agricultural production. But the urgency of the world food situation requires that, with the priorities in reverse order, all three be vigorously pursued.

Major recommendations are that:

THE UNFINISHED AGENDA

- **All forms of assistance be linked to bringing birth rates into line with death rates.**
- **A U.S.-Canada Commission on Food Policy be formed to guide the use of North American food in solving the world food shortage.**

The United States, already a leading producer of almost every agricultural commodity, will be taking steps to increase its output further. To increase total food production while decreasing adverse environmental impact and the drain on resources that are needed for other purposes, America must:

- **Restore and increase soil-conservation programs at the federal, state, and local levels.**
- **Stop the conversion of prime agricultural lands to other uses.**
- **Promote research and development of intermediate agricultural technologies, both for use at home and to aid agricultural development abroad.**
- **Recycle organic nutrients as a supplement to and partial substitute for chemical fertilizers, thus partially reducing the energy-intensiveness of American agriculture.**
- **Promote the use of biological methods of pest control.**

ENERGY

Like population and food, energy problems are global in scope. The number of nations now able to export energy has declined to only a few; for many, energy supplies are limited primarily to firewood and animal dung. The United States, once an exporter and now increasingly dependent on foreign suppliers, has a major role to play in the resolution of global energy problems. It is essential to devise and build a new type of energy economy far less dependent on dwindling supplies of gas and oil.

Introduction

A viable energy policy requires much elaboration, but the basic recommendations are:

- **To recognize that nuclear fission is rapidly dying as an energy option because of its high capital, environmental, social, and energy costs.**
- **To avoid the formidable economic and political costs of further electrification, make every effort to supply energy only in the quality needed for the task in hand.**
- **To inventory energy end-uses by quality needs, geographical clustering, and unit scale.**
- **To develop appropriately smaller-scale energy generation systems.**
- **To move rapidly from dependence on depletable energy capital to renewable energy income.**

High priority should be given to:

- **Intelligent coal technologies, both for direct combustion and for the local extraction of premium fluid fuels from coal.**
- **Solar space-conditioning.**
- **A dispersed fuel-alcohol industry.**
- **Integration of solid-waste management with energy and materials-recycling systems.**
- **Rejuvenation of urban mass transit and intercity railways.**
- **An overhaul of energy-intensive agriculture practices.**

Since none of these measures will succeed if conceived as purely technical, institutional barriers such as antique utility practices, mortgage regulations, and building codes, must be overcome. These reforms in turn rest on public understanding of their importance, enhanced by a more wide-ranging discussion of energy options and goals. Therefore:

- **Public participation, so far mainly formal, must become substantive.**
- **There must be a progressively increasing gasoline tax, the proceeds of which should be used to begin reducing the ill effects of automobiles.**

- **Mandatory fuel-economy standards must be maintained for automobiles and extended to other vehicles, including aircraft.**
- **Expansion of the interstate highway system must be discontinued and the funds and attention diverted to the nation's railroads.**
- **The 55 mph speed limit must be enforced through federal sanctions against states that do not comply.**
- **Subsidies to nuclear energy industries must be withdrawn and existing facilities phased out in orderly fashion.**
- **Utility price structures must be overhauled to reflect both policy priorities and sound economic principles.**
- **It will also be necessary to enforce antitrust and securities laws, so that alternative energy sources are not deprived of the benefits of competition and entrepreneurial vigor.**

NATURAL RESOURCES

The broad problem of energy supply implies a correspondingly broad problem of the availability of natural resources. The prosperity of the industrialized world, which has been built on abundant supplies of easily accessible energy and minerals, is now approaching a period of general scarcity. Therefore, it is recommended that:

- **The United States adopt as a long-range goal the achievement of a "Conserver Society," in which materials are used to maximum advantage with minimum resource depletion.**

Such a program would involve resource conservation, recycling, re-use, increased product durability, and long-term economic and social changes to minimize demand for materials in particularly short supply. We further recommend that:

Introduction

- The U.S. require that all goods sold in interstate commerce be labeled with disposal instructions.
- The principle be established that the sale price of manufactured products include disposal costs.
- The government adopt uniform legislation promoting recycling of beverage containers by requiring returnable deposits.
- Recycling of automobiles be promoted.
- Mandatory minimum standards be set for automobile durability.
- Special conservation and recycling measures be taken for scarce and critical elements whose future stocks are in question.

WATER AND AIR

There is no question that air and water pollution continue to pose serious problems for the nation, and although some progress has been made, available data are insufficient to assess fully the extent of progress or the effectiveness of present regulatory approaches.

- Better monitoring systems are needed as a management tool for the nation's very significant investments in air and water pollution control.

During 1977 Congress will be reviewing the Federal Water Pollution Control Act and the Clean Air Act Amendments. Ill omens for this process are already appearing.

- The integrity and goals of both of these Acts should be reaffirmed and defended against debilitating changes.
- EPA's air pollution research budget should be increased drastically for a comprehensive research program on the health effects of air pollution, especially toxic pollutants.

TOXIC SUBSTANCES

An intractable problem of modern industrial society is that of the pervasive presence of toxic chemicals. It is estimated that as much as 90 percent of human cancers are caused by environmental factors, including carcinogenic chemicals. Cancer is now the number-two killer of Americans, and is expected to develop in 25 percent of the U.S. population.

Cancer is not the only delayed health effect of concern to environmentalists. Many toxic substances are known to cause birth or genetic defects, learning disabilities, and behavioral disorders, while concentrations of toxic chemicals such as PCBs cause extensive contamination of natural ecosystems. Accordingly, we recommend that:

- **The Toxic Substances Control Act be implemented as fully as possible both for new chemicals and for those already in the environment.**
- **Special priority in research be given to filling gaps in scientific knowledge necessary for evaluating chemicals.**
- **Priorities in the National Cancer Plan be shifted to cancer prevention and away from the search for a cure for cancer.**
- **An all-out effort should be initiated to eliminate the single most significant cause of human cancer—tobacco smoke.**

THE LIFE-SUPPORT SYSTEM

The passengers together on the little spaceship Earth are not only beginning to harm the economic system; they are beginning to strain the entire life-support system of the spaceship, and to impinge on the health and welfare of other species, on whom it depends in ways more fundamental than is known. Some of man's activities are now on such a large scale that they are beginning to modify biogeochemical cycles and to change the physical or chemical bases of the global life-support system, producing regional or global effects. Of special concern are the effects of various pollutants on the ozone layer of the stratosphere.

It is recommended that:
- **Special efforts be taken to preserve endangered species on islands, especially Hawaii.**
- **U.S. efforts be continued to protect marine mammals.**
- **Congress act favorably on pending wilderness legislation.**
- **The provisions of the Endangered Species Act be better enforced.**
- **Increased funding be committed to allow proper management of public lands, especially National Parks.**
- **Congress act in 1977 to protect Alaskan wildlands.**
- **The 1872 Mining Law be drastically reformed or replaced with enlightened legislation.**
- **The urgently threatened ecosystems of U.S. lands be preserved and restored.**
- **Federal support be provided to State programs for regulation of areas of critical concern.**

In addition:
- **The United States must develop a worthy land ethic.**

NEW BIOLOGICAL THREAT

The possibility of creating new forms of life in the laboratory presents a monstrous threat to every species on earth. Using the recombinant DNA techniques, scientists can create new forms of life by cutting and splicing genes to transfer genetic material from one organism to another. Once successfully established, new forms of life are irreversible. The benefits to science are matched by unprecedented and unknown risks. A human epidemic would be the worst possible consequence, but massive outbreaks of crop disease or a major disturbance of the regional ecology could amount to nearly the same thing. For these compelling reasons, it is recommended that:

- **All laboratory efforts involving genetic engineering techniques be covered by the most comprehensive guidelines.**
- ***E. coli* be prohibited as host for recombinant DNA molecules.**
- **Appropriate health surveillance be made of laboratories.**
- **Recombinant DNA research be restricted to specific laboratories of the highest reputation, and training courses provided for all personnel.**
- **Certain experimental research be banned entirely.**

SOCIETY AND DECISION-MAKING

High inflation, unemployment, and growing dependence on foreign-oil imports have made it increasingly clear that all parts of the national socio-economic system are not working harmoniously toward any well-understood goal. Environmentalists believe these problems could be lessened by improved planning techniques, the management of technologies, and an economic and social transition to the intelligent use of resources.

First, since so many of the nation's problems require long-term solutions, we recommend that:

- **A full and active national discussion be launched immediately on how the nation can best develop a long-range planning capability.**

Second, since technologies have been developed (nuclear explosives, for example) with which single individuals could imperil large portions of our civilizations, it is necessary:

Introduction

- In the decade ahead not only to develop new controls over the application of existing technologies, but also to consider the full sociological implications of nascent technologies.

And third:

- **The environment must be recognized as a top national priority on a level with defense, employment, health, education, and commerce.**

To this end, there must be major changes in the U.S. economy, which would induce environmentally beneficial behavior and curb economically destructive practices while still preserving the meritorious aspects of free enterprise. Specific recommendations are that:

- **Antitrust laws be vigorously enforced.**
- **A program of legislation and economic sanction be initiated promptly against manufacturers who produce throw-away or unrepairable products, and who refuse to stock spare parts.**
- **A Presidential commission be established immediately to develop and recommend a more adequate set of national economic indicators.**
- **Research funds at the National Science Foundation and the Commerce Department be set aside and specifically earmarked for a study of a steady state economy to define the concept further and examine how best to manage it.**

The tendency of modern education to mold minds into narrow disciplinary specialties may be a root cause of modern environmental problems. Therefore it is recommended that:

- **Much further attention be given to education for environmental literacy, emphasizing causal relationships and feedback phenomena.**

Environmental literacy will also require attention to the content of the principal medium of continuing education—television. By the time the average youth graduates from high school, he will have spent 18,000 hours watching television—more time than it takes to earn a B.A. Television controls and sends out a message with unmistakable environmental consequences: Buy more products for self improvement.

Recognizing the influence of merchandising interests through the television medium, environmentalists recommend that:

- **The Council on Environmental Quality, with support from the National Science Foundation, undertake to monitor and analyze the explicit and implicit environmental message contained in both the programming and commercials on U.S. television.** The analysis should document clearly what is being said about environmental issues, resource consumption, pollution and lifestyles, and the implications for society if the viewing audience follows the example set by the role models on television.

Population: How Many Is Too Many?

1

THE MANY ELEMENTS THAT SUSTAIN our bodies and our civilizations cannot be sorted easily into neat lists or linear expositions—they tend to form circles and webs of interdependencies. Since the structure of our language is linear, this description of the environmental situation will have to proceed by setting one word after another. But the circular dependencies will become obvious: Energy will be relevant to food; fertilizers, necessary for the cultivation of food, will reappear under the headings of recycling and of clear water; and the question of land use will affect food, wilderness preservation, even the life of our oceans. Since the discussion must start somewhere, it will begin with population, one of the most basic sources of both problems and solutions to problems.

POPULATION GROWTH

Census, birth, and death statistics around the world are so uncertain that the human population can only be estimated at best with 10 percent accuracy. World population has been growing exponentially with a doubling time estimated to be between thirty-five and forty years. If this rate were to continue, the current world population of about 4 billion would reach 8 billion soon after the year 2000. The number of people added to the world population in 1976 is expected to be at least 64 million, most of whom will be members of poor families in poor nations. Given the momentum of current growth rates, the lowest UN projections show world population approaching at least 10 to 16 billion before leveling off.

In three geographic regions—Western Europe, North America, and East Asia (principally China)—population growth rates (but not populations) declined steadily during the first half of the 70s.[1] In Western Europe, the annual rate of population increase declined from .56 percent in 1970 to .32 percent in 1975, reducing the growth rate of this region by nearly one-half. If this declining trend continues, population in this region will be stabilized by the end of the current decade. In East Asia the growth rate declined from about 1.8 percent to 1.2 percent—an achievement all the more impressive since East Asia has by far the largest population (in terms of people per square mile) of any geographic region.

In North America the population growth rates of the United States and Canada have been declining slightly, although both populations are still growing. Thus some progress is being made, although the problem is far from resolved. On May 1, 1976, the United States population totaled about 215 million and was increasing at the rate of 0.8 percent per year, or 1,700,000 persons per year. Net legal immigration accounted for about 20 percent of this increase, or 350,000 persons per year. The remaining increment of 1,350,000 persons per year comes from natural increase, the excess of births over deaths. These increase rates have been roughly stable (except for seasonal trends) over the last four years. The figures do not, however, take illegal immigration into account; this subject will be discussed later.

For the past few years the fertility rate for American families has been slightly lower than that necessary for population replacement, in the absence of immigration. Total fertility rate has been about 1.8 children per woman.[2] Population replacement calls for 2.1 children per woman. *If* this fertility rate and the current mortality rate should continue for about fifty years (and if there were no illegal immigration), the U.S. population would gradually stop growing and begin to decline. The stabilization and slow decrease would not take place for some time because the higher fertility of Americans during the 1950s and 1960s has produced a large baby-boom generation that is just moving into its reproductive years. Even if these young couples have on the average fewer children than the generation before them, the number of new babies is likely to be higher, because there are more childbearing couples. This bump of young people in the population is thus likely to produce more births than deaths and a growing population for several decades to come, even if fertility rates remain at the present low level.

There is no guarantee, of course, that American fertility will remain where it is now. Historically the average fertility rates of the developed-country populations, including the United States, have fluctuated between slightly less than two and somewhat over three children per family. The fluctuations seem to parallel the business cycle; fertility goes up during prosperous periods, down during economic recessions.[3] The actual growth path is more likely to be somewhere between 300 and 400 million in 2015 if the birth rate continues to fluctuate as it has in the past.[4]

Governments influence population growth rates every time they influence the economic and social conditions relevant to individual families. Such governmental functions as taxation, housing policy, public health administration, highway construction, and education all affect family incomes, expectations, costs, and location—

and thus affect childbearing decisions. There is no question that government policy can influence birth and death rates. The question is only whether that influence will be accidental and unpredictable or deliberate and consistent with other social policies. At present it is accidental—there is no coordinated U.S. population policy, although the President's Commission on Population Growth and the American Future recommended in 1972 that there should be one.

A population policy for the U.S. should strive to achieve two goals. The first goal would be to increase the *quality* of life for the American population, whatever its size, by seeking to foster a stable family environment that will insure that each child is born into a life of sufficiency, freedom, and opportunity and into a stable, loving human environment. Hardly anyone would oppose such a goal, and several programs to achieve it are already in existence. These include many welfare programs, family planning, maternal, and child health programs, and a variety of educational endeavors. A second goal would be to reduce the ultimate size of the American population by encouraging fertility levels as low as or even lower than present levels and by reviewing the scope of immigration in light of U.S. population. Such a policy has never been officially adopted by this country, and it probably would be questioned by many who do not see its connection to the first goal. The arguments in favor of attempting to stabilize the U.S. population at a reasonably small size are:

(1) All else being equal, a larger population will mean less access per person to most economic and environmental resources. Ocean beaches, wilderness areas, and prime agricultural lands are simply not expandable: more people can only mean greater scarcity of these resources. Supplies of other resources, such as minierals, land, and energy, can possibly be maintained, but only at increasing cost.

> If . . . we choose to have more rather than less children per family . . . we commit ourselves to a particular package of problems: more rapid depletion of domestic and international resources, greater pressures on the environment, more dependence on continued rapid technological development to solve these problems, fewer social options and perhaps the continued postponement of other social problems, including those resulting from past growth.[5]

Thus the stabilization, or even gradual reduction, of the U.S. population seems to be a step in the direction of increased quality of life for Americans.

(2) An active, sincere effort to stabilize U.S. population could increase the credibility of our aid to family planning programs abroad. Third World countries have been quick to point out that each new American consumes five times as much food and sixty times as much energy per year as the average South Asian. Thus the 1,300,000 Americans added each year through natural increase constitute at least as much of a burden on the global resource base as the annual increase of 12,000,000 in India. If Americans are serious about solving the global problems of poverty, environmental deterioration, and resource depletion, they could begin by putting their own house in order.

(3) Finally, there seems to be no very good reason to encourage population growth. It does not seem to be necessary to stimulate the economy (West Germany's population is now slowly decreasing, while its economy is sound). A market of 215 million people seems to make possible any economies of scale imaginable. Modern warfare depends less on numbers of soldiers than on technology and resources. The country has been settled from shore to shore. All the traditional reasons for the state to encourage population growth have become obsolete.

A FOURFOLD PROGRAM

What actual policies, programs, and efforts might the government undertake to promote the goals of preventing the birth of unwanted babies and strengthening the family while stabilizing or decreasing population quantity? The list of possible measures can be divided into four main categories. First come policies to augment options and freedoms, to let people follow their own reproductive goals by removing present constraints that bind them to a narrow range of behavior. Second are policies to strengthen the family, to increase, as far as government can, the care, knowledge, resources, and love with which each child is raised. These first two categories are directed toward improved quality of the human life experience and should be implemented whatever the national concern about population size. Two further categories deal with policies for stabilizing or reducing population numbers; they address the questions of desired family size and of immigration.

Increasing choices

In a society that is trying to produce a smaller number of children and to give those fewer children more love and more opportunities, the first priority is clearly to prevent the conception and birth of unplanned, unwanted children.

Nearly 1 million teenagers become pregnant each year in the United States. Approximately two-thirds of these pregnancies are carried to delivery, the others are aborted. Most of these conceptions are unplanned and unwanted and many result in marriages that have only a 50-50 chance of lasting even five years. This "epidemic" of unwanted births is due to increased sexual activity, non-use or ineffective use of contraceptives, and lack of contraceptive information and services for teenagers. Only one-fifth to one-third of the teenagers in need of contraceptive services and information are being served by organized programs. Teenagers tend to believe that they cannot become pregnant easily; this belief reveals their ignorance about reproduction. Teenagers are more likely to have complications related to pregnancy, and their children face substantial health risks. High rates of infant mortality, prematurity, low birth weights, and child abuse are common. Despite gains made in liberalizing laws regarding contraception and abortion for minors, unmarried teenagers in many communities still have trouble locating the services they need.

Governmental policies that would improve fertility control include:

- **Increased support for established family planning organizations.**
- **Support for clinics that provide contraceptives, pregnancy testing, abortion and sterilization.**
- **Sex and family education programs, especially for pre-teens and teenagers (further explored under "Strengthening the family" below.**

In a few years great strides have been made in equalizing employment opportunities and wages for women. But a major social change of this sort must be pursued for at least a generation before it becomes fully established. Every effort should be made to:

- **Encourage and publicize role models so that young girls regularly see women in all sorts of social occupations, including positions of responsibility and authority.**

Equality for the only child, the unmarried, and the childless is important. The norm in our society is to get married and to have two or three children; deviation from the norm is still punished by subtle forms of social pressure. Since children growing up should consider

childlessness or the small family real options for their own lives, we recommend:
- **Positive publicity for those who have chosen not to marry or to have children.**
- **Emphasis on the creative possibilities opened up by freedom from the heavy responsibilities of a large family.**
- **Removal of taxation discriminations against such life choices.**

Strengthening the family

Strengthening the family and increasing its ability to nurture, love, and educate future generations are matters of national concern since they determine the ultimate human resources upon which the nation depends. Measures to strengthen the family could include:
- **Education for family life,** including not only sex education but an understanding of all that is required for stable marriage and responsible parenthood, from budget-balancing to meal-planning, from health care to cooperation. Some experimental programs of this sort exist, and include, for example, visits to the mortgage department of a bank and to a pediatrician, and sessions of actual baby care. Such education can help young people to enter marriage and parenthood with more realistic expectations and with some of the many skills necessary for family life.
- **Day-care facilities, paternity as well as maternity leaves, flexible work schedules and other such measures that permit coordination of parenthood duties with other career duties.** Too often the conflict between the responsibilities of family and career results in the breakup of the family, to the detriment of the children.

Another measure that should be considered is welfare payments to indigent families in kind rather than in cash, especially providing for children's needs, such as nutritious food, clothing, books and other educational materials, and health care.

Desired family size

Such measures would enable Americans to envision and choose among a number of lifestyles and to plan and have the number of children they find consistent with their own personal goals and constraints. They would, however, not guarantee that the aggregate average family size will be low enough to stabilize or decrease population. Throughout history governments have been notoriously ineffective in directly influencing desired family size. Any information provided by governments to families should promote the public good and

> ... should be honest, should start from the true interest of the individual himself, and in any case should not divert him from clear thinking about his own values and motives. ... The state should appear for what it is and voice the reasons it has as the collectivity of individuals for wanting more or fewer children.[6]

In order to keep desired family size around the replacement level of two children per family, the government could:
- **Declare a national goal of population stabilization or gradual population decrease,** and indicate to the public the national benefits to be gained from such a goal.
- **Encourage public education in demography and ecology,** so that the general principles of exponential growth, carrying capacity, and the social impact of individual reproductive decisions become widely known.

- **Establish the small family as a desirable and socially responsible ideal** via public information programs.
- **Remove current pronatalist incentives, such as income-tax exemptions, for third-and-beyond children.**

Immigration

For the first time since the early 1900s, legal and illegal immigration to the United States has during 1974 and 1975 equaled or even exceeded the natural increase in population (births minus deaths). In particular, the flow of illegal immigrants to the United States, largely from Latin America and the Caribbean, has climbed sharply upward since 1970.[7]

Legal immigration to the U.S. during 1975 was estimated officially at about 500,000 (including Vietnam refugees). By conservative estimate illegal immigration contributed another 800,000 to make a total of at least 1,300,000.

Immigration into the United States may help unskilled individuals fleeing the scarcity of food, jobs, and housing, but legal immigration into the U.S. usually siphons off skilled people—particularly physicians—badly needed at home. Both skilled and unskilled immigrants may have significant impacts upon the wages, job conditions, and unemployment among resident U.S. workers. Small wonder that organized labor is concerned with immigration.

If the present U.S. fertility level remains constant (below replacement) and the present legal and illegal immigration rates are maintained, the population will reach 282 million by the year 2000, and will go on growing indefinitely after that. On the other hand, if fertility remained constant, illegal immigration were stopped, and legal migration continued at current rates, the population in 2000 would be 254 million and the population would

Population

stabilize in 2025. Illegal entry into the United States should, therefore, be ended, and legal immigration reduced to a level approximating emigration. Specific plans for accomplishing this should include:

- **Increased funding for and efficiency within the agencies that administer immigration policy.**
- **Criminal penalties against those who knowingly employ illegal aliens** coupled with measures to end the abuse of Social Security cards, to protect the jobs of citizens and legal alien residents.
- **Gradual reduction of quotas for legal immigration** with the exception of immediate families of citizens and resident aliens, refugees and orphans.
- **Economic development assistance to foreign countries** which are potential sources of illegal aliens, to remove the root causes of immigration.
- **Adoption by Congress of a policy statement on immigration,** which relates immigration to national population, resources, employment, and education policies.
- **Assistance for legal migrants** to help them with language and employment problems.

These measures, if implemented, could bring to a close the era of demographically significant immigration into the United States.

Food and Agriculture

2

DURING THE 1950S AND 60S, the world agricultural system produced more food than could be sold.[1] During these decades of food surplus, world population growth climbed to its highest rate ever. Whenever famine threatened, it was checked by food aid, as in 1966 and 1967 when a fifth of the U.S. wheat crop went to sustain India through a drought.

During the early 70s the situation changed markedly. World demand for food outstripped the capacity of the world farmers and fishermen to produce. Both per capita food production and per capita fish catch turned downward. As production fell behind demand, food stocks were depleted, and idle crop land was returned to use. At its lowest point, the world carry-over stores of grain were capable of meeting demand for less than one month. In 1972 there was an absolute decline in food production of 3 percent, the first absolute decline in total output in two decades.

In some parts of the world food shortages are already severe enough to interfere with population growth by raising death rates, at least in years of bad weather.[2] In the poverty-ridden state of Uttar Pradesh in northern India, for example, the death rate climbed from 20.1 per 1000 in 1971 to 25.6 in 1972 following a poor harvest. In the smaller states of Bihar and Orissa, data for 1972 suggest that an additional 235,000 and 101,000 lives were lost respectively. In these three Indian states alone, hunger claimed an estimated 829,000 lives that year. Nationwide the decrease in food supplies in 1972 probably claimed well over a million lives.

The impact of food shortages on the people of Bangladesh has been even more severe than in India. During 1971–72, food production in Bangladesh was affected both by the insurrection, associated with the move toward independence in Pakistan, and by adverse growing conditions. Data for Matlab Bazar Thana District, kept by the International Cholera Research Laboratory, indicate that the death rate climbed from an average of 15.3 for the 1966–70 period to 21.4 in the 1971–72 period. If it is assumed that these data are representative of the entire country, then an extrapolation suggests an increase in deaths of 427,000. A Ford Foundation report notes that the average food consumption dropped from about 15 ounces daily in the 60s to a near-starvation level of 12 ounces in 1971.

In areas such as these pressures of population may actually undermine and destroy major food-producing systems.[3] This is most evident in ocean fisheries and in countries with fragile ecosystems such as the Sahelian zone countries of Africa, the countries of the East African plateau, particularly Ethiopia, and mountainous countries such as Nepal and the Andean areas of Latin America.

Continuing explosive rates of population growth could lead to a collapse of whole regional food production systems, a dangerous prospect especially since the world's climate also seems to be changing for the worse.

There is considerable evidence that weather patterns from 1900 to about 1970 were unusually favorable for agriculture.[4] The climatological norm is defined as the period between 1930 and 1960, but Reed Bryson, a world renowned climatologist, points out that what is now termed "normal" is perhaps the most abnormal period in a thousand years—that is, abnormally mild. The warmest years occurred in the 1940s, and a cooling trend has subsequently set in, a trend made much of in the media and often blamed for the weather troubles in 1972 and 1974.

The result of these simultaneous trends—rising populations increasing the demand for food and a worsening climate possibly interfering with supply—will be worldwide food scarcity and it is to be expected with increasing frequency in the future, in large regions of the world. By one estimate,[5] South Asia will require 500 million tons of grain imports in the year 2025. This amount is twice the present North American grain crop and, even if it were available, is twice as much as the total tonnage of *all goods* now being shipped overseas from the United States.

More food of course can and will be raised in the world, at increasing economic and environmental cost. And sufficient food to support the present population does now exist. If it were equally distributed, this year's global food production could feed 4 billion people adequately. The actual inequality of distribution and the increasing dominance of North America in world food trade are illustrated by the following table of global imports and exports of grain (grains occupy more than 70 percent of the world's cropland area):

Food and Agriculture

THE CHANGING PATTERN OF WORLD GRAIN TRADE[6]

Region	1934-38	1948-52	1960	1970	1976[b]
	(Million metric tons)				
North America	+5[a]	+23	+39	+56	+94
Latin America	+9	+1	0	+4	−3
Western Europe	−24	−22	−25	−30	−17
E. Europe & U.S.S.R.	+5	—	0	0	−27
Africa	+1	0	−2	−5	−10
Asia	+2	−6	−17	−37	−47
Australia & New Zealand	+3	+3	+6	+12	+8

Source: The Worldwatch Institute, derived from FAO and USDA data.
[a]Plus sign indicates net exports; minus sign, net imports.
[b]Preliminary estimates of fiscal year data.

There are basically only three possible approaches[7] to the world food problem: increase food production, redistribute more effectively the food that is already grown, and stabilize the world population growth that is increasing food demand. U.S. policy currently emphasizes the first of these, through agricultural research, economic aid and agricultural assistance, and export of surplus agricultural production. The U.S. has recently begun promoting some efforts toward redistribution by working within world forums to develop a global buffer stock program to store grains in time of surplus, to be used in time of need. Efforts toward population control on a global scale consist primarily of distribution of family-planning information and contraceptive devices.

The world food situation is sufficiently critical that all three of these areas of activity should be pursued, each one more vigorously than it is now. And a reversal of priorities is necessary. Population stabilization is the *only* possible long-term solution and the one with the fewest economic and environmental costs (though it may have significant social costs). Redistribution should come next in importance, for moral reasons, as well as economic and environmental ones. Increasing food production will certainly be necessary in the short term, but it should be considered the least desirable of the three programs.

INTERNATIONAL POPULATION CONTROL

The first priority is stabilization of the U.S. population, which could well be the single most effective thing this country could do to promote global population control efforts. Beyond that, involvement with population matters in another country must be handled carefully, discreetly, and only at the invitation of the other country. Measures to be considered include:

- **Continuation and increased funding of family planning programs, research into fertility control methods, and training of paramedical personnel in recipient nations** to administer and follow up on simple techniques of contraception, sterilization, and abortion.
- **Technical and data-processing assistance to any nation desiring to improve its methods of census or vital statistic registration, or to conduct resource surveys, or to do long-range population planning.**
- **Special emphasis on foreign aid measures that have an indirect negative effect on fertility, such as female education, female employment, or social security programs.**
- **Relating all forms of assistance to the necessity of bringing birth rates into line with death rates.**

U.S. policy should be insistent upon one simple condition: that birth rates shall not be maintained higher than death rates. That constraint is derived from the physical laws of the planet, however, not from the selfish desires of any one group of people. This condition for population stabilization may interfere with some freedoms, but it lets each government accomplish that interference as it sees fit. At the same time it creates other freedoms by reducing the threats to survival, welfare, and equity that overpopulation would bring.

REDISTRIBUTION OF FOOD SUPPLIES

Two methods of distribution are possible: emergency food distribution systems to assemble food stocks and utilize them as efficiently as possible during times of famine, and more long-term distribution schemes to achieve a better permanent balance between food demand and food production. The recommendations here focus on the more long-term approach, since several excellent proposals already exist and are being worked out to improve the world's ability to respond to short-term food problems.

To achieve a more equitable distribution of the world's food resources, we recommend the formation of:

- **A U.S.-Canada Commission on Food Policy to use North American food to support efforts for solving the world food shortage.**[8]

In a very limited sense, the efforts of this Joint Commission would parallel those by the OPEC countries to manage petroleum, though neither the objectives nor the techniques would be at all similar. OPEC used the price mechanism and production controls to increase dramatically the export earnings of member countries. But oil price hikes, by focusing global attention on the prospective exhaustion of oil reserves within the next few decades, emphasized the urgent need both to conserve petroleum and to devise alternative energy sources.

The ground rules for assured access to North American food markets should be understood as support of the World Plan of Action on population agreed to at the UN Population Conference in Bucharest in August 1974 and the international food strategy agreed upon at Rome. For example, participants in the UN World Food Conference in Rome agreed that all countries should provide current reliable information on crop conditions and food reserves. Within months after the food conference, the Soviet Union, acting under a shroud of secrecy, was purchasing grain on a massive scale in flagrant violation of this strategy. These secretive, erratic, massive Soviet purchases are a major source of instability in the world food economy.

A joint U.S.-Canada Food Commission could insist that only those countries that support the internationally accepted strategy to solve the world food problem through responsible national actions can have access to North American food. Those countries in which agriculture is stagnating or lagging will need to reform their agricultural sectors and do whatever is necessary to get production moving. All countries should be required to be explicit about their own food reserve goals and the specific steps they are taking to achieve them. Those countries not following the World Plan of Action of 1974 and not contributing to the stabilization of world population should not count on access to North American food supplies. In effect, access to North American food supplies should be used as an incentive to encourage and assist countries to do their share in solving the food problem, and thereby to help avoid an unmanageable, potentially catastrophic food crisis.

- **Reduce unnecessarily wasteful levels of food consumption in the U.S.**

If the United States hopes to persuade other countries to follow long-term, globally-oriented population and food policies, it should actively try to reduce consumption of food-related commodities, including fertilizer and energy. Measures to be considered include luxury taxes on grain-fed meat, tobacco, or highly processed foods;

limitation of fertilizer use to agricultural purposes; control of pet populations; nutrition education; and numerous energy-conservation measures, from minimum fuel-efficiency standards for automobiles to deregulation of natural gas and petroleum prices. These measures would do more than increase the international credibility of the United States. They would also improve domestic economic health by reducing dependence on imports of vital resources, and by hastening the coming technological transition from nonrenewable to renewable resources.

- **To the extent possible, encourage the reduction of direct donations of food to poor countries.**

Domestic conservation policies could increase the large amount of food the United States has available for sale on the world market. Some of this surplus should be allocated to grain buffer stocks for countering weather-induced emergencies. As far as possible, the remainder should be sold on the international market, not given away. Donated food provides short-term aid to poor countries, but at the same time it destroys local incentives, encourages corruption, and tends to undermine the economic development of local agriculture without providing an incentive for lowering birth rates.

- **Promote economic development, especially agricultural development, of the poorer countries, so that they can move toward food self-sufficiency.**

Reduction in food aid does not imply reduction in other kinds of aid or disinterest in the plight of the poor. On the contrary, if food-importing countries are to benefit from U.S. surplus on the international market, they must have purchasing power derived from their own economic systems. The development of those economic systems can be hastened by foreign aid, but not by direct transfers of Western food, capital, or technology. Two directions of change in U.S. aid policy might lead to a fair and permanent global redistribution of economic power.

First, a new attitude about the way the United States

provides development aid to other countries might be useful. Current examination of several past decades of foreign aid is resulting in a healthy skepticism about the general applicability of Western methods, resources, and organizational forms to non-Western societies. Out of this reassessment should come not discouragement and abandonment of effort, but a constructive humility and openness to other ways of doing things. If the United States could approach the problem of each country's development as a co-explorer, willing to listen and learn as well as to teach, it might be more welcome, and might also make more progress. Second, a more systematic understanding of the distributional consequences of international trade is needed. The Third World countries have often complained that the international terms of trade discriminate against them. This is true; recent studies confirm that the operations of multinational corporations[9] and of the world food market[10] both result in an effective subsidy to the rich nations from the poor. If the international economic system regularly undermines what aid programs are attempting to do, then a restructuring of trade as well as aid would certainly be in order.

INCREASING AGRICULTURAL PRODUCTION

The United States could surely produce more food and help other countries to produce more food. Although this country is a leading producer of almost every agricultural commodity, its agricultural dominance is due more to a low population density and an endowment of good agricultural land and temperate climate than it is to superior management of agricultural resources. On a list of the twenty major world food crops and the nations that regularly achieve the highest yield per acre of each, the United States does not appear even once.[11] The question is whether the environmental and economic costs of producing more food would be tolerable. The following suggestions deal with ways of using our agricultural lands and the other resources in a way that will increase total food production while decreasing adverse environmental impact and the drain on resources that are needed for other purposes.

During the past 200 years, about 236 million acres of U.S. farmland have been lost from production, an area half as large as that now under cultivation.[12] Most of this loss has been to erosion, the rest to "development." In the past few decades the rate of loss to development has increased markedly, and it is expected to increase even faster in the next few decades as the baby boom population forms new households. Two policies are needed, one to reduce erosion and one to divert development away from agricultural lands:

- **Restore and increase soil conservation programs at the federal, state, and local levels.** A number of excellent anti-erosion programs were instituted as a reaction to the dust-bowl problems of the 1930s and then languished during the surplus-production years of the 1960s. Soil conservation requires constant vigilance, not merely the on-again, off-again efforts that fluctuate with market conditions. A few years of neglect may destroy topsoil that took hundreds of years to form. A review of the old soil-conservation programs should be undertaken, and the lessons learned from their successes and failures used to design a new set of programs that will consistently aid farmers in building up and maintaining the fertility of prime agricultural land, while maintaining the diversity and productivity of marginal wetlands and uncultivated lands.
- **Stop the conversion of prime agricultural lands into other uses.**

America's best farmlands are flat, well-drained, and not far from major population centers. Unfortunately such land is also best for all sorts of building purposes, from shopping centers to subdivisions. Sensible land-use planning would divert development to marginal lands where construction costs may be higher but where development could easily proceed without affecting agricultural production. The ultimate solution is strict zoning on either the federal or the state level to conserve prime agricultural land for agricultural purposes only. This sort of zoning is already in effect in nearly every European country. As discussed later, reform of the property-tax system to assess land at the value of actual (rather than potential) use would eliminate much of the pressure for development of farmlands near urban areas.

● **Promote research and development of intermediate agricultural technologies, both for use at home and to aid agricultural development abroad.**

Intermediate agricultural technology emphasizes tools and inputs that are appropriate for villages and small farms and that can be manufactured and repaired locally from renewable materials. It also involves more human and less fossil fuel energy. Examples of these intermediate technologies include digesters to produce fertilizers from household and urban organic wastes, biological pest control, windmills for pumping water, solar grain driers, small sturdy hand tractors, methane generators, and many sorts of handtools. Some of these suggestions may sound like a return to old-fashioned practices. But new designs, materials, and knowledge are now being combined with traditional methods in some ingenious attempts to capture the best of the new and the old.[13]

Intermediate technologies are ideally suited for nonindustrialized countries with excess labor and a shortage of capital. They naturally conserve commodities whose prices are now rising, such as petroleum and natural gas. Ecologically, intermediate technologies are much more acceptable than current Western farming methods. Besides combating erosion and gradually improving soil fertility, they tend to introduce fewer foreign substances into ecosystems, since they are based on naturally-occurring renewable materials.

The intermediate scale is fully compatible with redistribution goals that call for smaller farms. Neither intermediate-technology farming nor smaller units of production are likely to reduce output. In many countries smaller farms consistently outproduce large farms on a per acre basis, although they do produce less output per man-hour.[14] In other words, they maximize returns to increasingly scarce factors of production, namely land and energy, rather than to an increasingly abundant one— labor. These production methods are capable therefore of producing both increased total output and increased rural employment. The energy used in food production has been increasing faster than energy use in many other sectors of the world economy.[15] For example, Pimentel and associates documented that while yields doubled from 1945 to 1970, energy inputs in U.S. corn production more than *tripled*. In 1970 the energy input for nitrogen fertilizer alone about equalled the total energy inputs for corn production in 1945. Nitrogen, fertilizers, machinery, and fuel inputs now account for about two-thirds of all the energy inputs in corn production.

In the United States today about 3 kilocalories (kcal) of food energy is returned per input of 1 kcal of fossil fuel energy. By comparison, about 130 kcal of food energy is returned per 1 kcal of fossil energy when corn is produced by more labor-intensive methods.

A further complication in considering the energy intensiveness of U.S. agriculture is the fact that most corn and other cereal grains do not serve as human food but instead are fed to livestock. Of the estimated 1,600 lbs of grain per capita utilized in the U.S., only about 6 percent (140 lbs) is consumed directly by humans. Most of the cereal grains are fed to livestock; the livestock in turn becomes food. The U.S. annual per capita animal protein consumption (250 lbs) is one of the highest in the world.

Because animals must be fed vegetable protein for their production, the conversion of vegetable to animal protein has a high "energy cost." Between 5 and 10 lbs of grain and fish protein are fed to livestock on feedlots to obtain an additional 1 lb of beef. Translated into energy inputs, this means about 10 times as much fossil energy is necessary to produce a calorie of animal protein than to produce a calorie of plant protein. Range-fed beef produce protein from grass with only very limited fossil fuels required, but under feedlot conditions about 78 kcal of fossil energy are required per kcal of beef protein produced.

Given the high protein and calorie diet consumed in the U.S., along with its energy-intensive food production, processing, distribution, and preparation system, an estimated 15 percent of the energy utilized in our economy is used in the food system. About 5 percent is used in production, about 5 percent for processing, and about 5 percent for distribution and preparation.

On the surface, this 15 percent for food may not appear to be much, compared with the energy costs of other sectors of our economy. (In gasoline equivalents this is about 330 gallons per capita per year, or 70 billion gallons annually in the United States.) Yet the astounding fact is that this 330 gallons for food represents twice the total energy inputs expended per capita for all purposes in the developing countries.

The energy-intensivity of the agriculture sector may be reduced in many ways without reducing agricultural yields. Most of the necessary changes will occur eventually as the price of energy increases but will be hastened if the price supports that keep energy artificially inexpensive are removed. Examples of simple changes that will substitute human labor for fossil-fuel energy in agriculture (and increase jobs) are use of the sun instead of propane to dry grains, use of smaller-size mechanical equipment (which would also be more appropriate on smaller-size farms), and especially use of natural, sun-powered mechanisms for building soil fertility and for controlling insects. These latter two recommendations are so important that they are discussed in more detail.

THE CHEMICAL FERTILIZER PROBLEM

Our recommendation here is to:
- **Recyle organic nutrients as a supplement to and partial substitute for chemical fertilizers.**

This recommendation would have three desirable effects: It would reduce energy use in the production of fertilizers, it would reduce the many adverse environmental effects of fertilizers, and it would solve a major solid-waste problem—the disposal of urban garbage and sewage sludge. There is *no evidence* that replacing chemical fertilizers with organic fertilizers would reduce crop yields; in fact every comparative study that has been performed indicates that organically-operated farms yield as well as or better than farms that use only chemical fertilizers,[16] if sufficient organic fertilizer is available. The Chinese experience also supports this conclusion, but there is growing evidence that the People's Republic has insufficient organic fertilizer to satisfy its needs for fixed nitrogen.

Aside from their expense and energy content, artificially manufactured plant nutrients—such as urea, ammonia, and superphosphates—have many undesirable environmental effects. Most important, they seem to reduce the populations of natural fertility-producing organisms in the soil, such as earthworms and nitrogen-fixing bacteria. Thus they become addictive; as the natural (and free) nutrient-producing processes are reduced, more and more man-made (and costly) nutrients must be added to soil. Second, the man-made fertilizers are very soluble in water—that is why they are so effective so quickly, but it is also why they are quickly washed off the soil and into fresh water supplies, where they cause eutrophication and accumulation of nitrogen compounds poisonous in high concentrations to humans. Fertilizer runoff is the major source of non-point water pollution, a fact that will be discussed later. Finally, increasing numbers of scientists around the world are becoming persuaded that the overuse of nitrogen fertilizers is contributing to the release of oxides of nitrogen, which in turn react in the upper atmosphere to deplete the layer of ozone which protects the earth from the sun's ultraviolet light. Increased ultraviolet light would contribute to growing numbers of skin cancers throughout the world and would produce serious adverse effects on the very plants that humans depend on for their food.

Furthermore, there is an alternative to chemical fertilizers. At the same time that they are causing environmental problems, costing money, and using energy, natural fertilizers in the form of sewage sludge, feedlot manures, and urban garbage are *not* being used on the land, and therefore are causing environmental problems, costing money, and using energy. These natural fertilizers could be composted and returned to the land instead of being dumped or incinerated (the few cities and towns, such as Milwaukee, Wisconsin, that do compost their organic wastes and sell them as fertilizer find that this process pays for their entire sewage and garbage systems). Organic fertilizers are dissolved only slowly, at about the rate that plants can take them up, so they do not contribute heavily to water pollution.

It is not yet certain that all the plant nutrients needed for American agriculture could be supplied by recycled organic materials. Probably some judicious use of chemical fertilizers would always be needed, just as they are in

China. What is certain is that a much higher fraction of current fertilizer needs could be supplied by organics, thus solving several environmental problems in the process. It is also certain that techniques for safe processing and distributing of organic nutrients would be of great value to developing countries, who are trying simultaneously to increase food production and to improve primitive systems of dealing with human sewage.

- **Promote the use of biological methods of pest control.**

Some commercial farmers as well as millions of backyard gardeners in the United States never use toxic pesticides or herbicides. They do use sophisticated methods of pest control, including natural predators, careful timing of planting, destruction of alternate hosts, and interspersing plants with insect-repellent properties, such as marigolds, garlic, onions, and herbs. These methods may turn out to be more labor-intensive than spraying with toxic pesticides, but the yields are high and the effect on the environment is far more beneficial. The presence of pesticide residues in food and the effect of these residues on ecological systems are both major problems. Pesticides are expensive and energy-intensive. Many non-toxic, cheap, natural pest-control methods are already available.[8] Many more can and should be discovered.

The Energy Economy

3

ENERGY PROBLEMS, like those of population and food, are global in scope. Only a few nations now are still able to export energy; for many others, energy supplies are limited primarily to firewood and animal dung. The United States—once an exporter, and now increasingly dependent on foreign suppliers, most of whom belong to OPEC—has a major role to play in the resolution of global energy problems.

It is essential to devise and build a new type of energy economy far less dependent on dwindling supplies of fluid fuels. As conservationists had forewarned, several years ago the United States used up most of its easily accessible reserves of domestic oil and gas. These essential fluid fuels are now found increasingly in remote and hostile places at ever greater difficulty, cost, and risk. Within a few decades, world extraction of oil and gas will also peak and start to decline. As it is, this country is rapidly becoming reliant on imports from a single, politically volatile region, to the detriment of both our economic and political independence. This change in fortune caught the government largely by surprise. Therefore it is imperative that the United States devise a new energy plan.

THE CURRENT DILEMMA

The concerns of environmentalists can best be conveyed by taking a close look at the current plan (the initial draft of which was presented optimistically in late 1974 under the title Project Independence) and then comparing it with a possible alternative policy.[1]

Project Independence and its later drafts assume rapidly growing supplies of energy, especially in the form of electricity, to be essential to a healthy economy. Increased efficiency in using energy is thought desirable. Yet the resources and initiative to be devoted to increased efficiency are slight, and effective action has a low priority in government. The most important institutional barriers to increased end-use efficiency remain undisturbed, while modestly higher prices are assumed to provide a vague, generalized incentive to conserve energy (mainly in industry). Prices are not to rise to levels that reflect true costs, and billions of dollars per year in taxpayer subsidies continue to be poured into the energy industry.[2] No fundamental overhaul of the methods of energy production or the patterns of energy consumption is envisaged.

In the government's plan, all domestic fuel resources are to be heavily drawn upon in a program that has been described as one of "strength through exhaustion." Enhanced recovery of oil and gas in conventional wells is to be rapidly supplemented by new offshore and Alaskan wells. Nearly 1,000 such offshore wells in the continental United States are projected to be in operation by the mid-1980s. Public and private lands in the West are to be opened to an enormous expansion of coal-mining, mainly by strip-mining. New synthetic-fuel industries, railways, slurry pipelines, and clusters of giant coal-fired power stations are to be built. Underground and strip-mines in the East are also to be greatly expanded: by the year 2000 there would be perhaps 1,000 to 1,600 new coal mines, producing coal at a rate two or three times that of today.

A major new industry to mine and process Western oil shale is projected. By 2000 there would be 450 to 800 large nuclear reactors operating, including perhaps 80 fast breeders. These will require a vast associated network of reprocessing and fabrication plants, new enrichment capacity, and hundreds of new uranium mines (if the uranium can indeed be found). The electrical grid would more than double by 1985, then more than redouble by 2000—with a capacity for operating some 15 million private electric cars and for other uses.[3]

The Office of Technology Assessment and other critics have pointed out fundamental flaws in Project Independence:

(1) It cannot prevent inevitable and worsening shortages of fluid fuels, because the electricity to which three-fourths of the investment would be devoted cannot readily substitute for fluid fuels.

(2) There would be a tremendous drain on available capital. The capital intensity of the synthetic-fuel and electrical technologies proposed is respectively about ten and a hundred times that of the direct-fuel systems of this country's traditional industrial economy. Over the next decade, for example, the 1975 version of Project Independence would cost over a trillion of today's dollars. It would require not only the usual quarter of all net private domestic investment devoted to the energy sector but also about two-thirds of the remaining moneys available for all investments from the private sector.

(3) The efficiency of converting raw fuels into delivered energy would steadily decline, resulting in an enormous waste of energy within the energy industry itself. Fixed distribution costs already account for half of the consumer's electricity bill.

(4) Even with the best practices and safeguards, the direct impact of the new energy system on land, water, air, and human communities would be enormously destruc-

tive. To mention but a few problems: oil spills with potentially disastrous biological or climatic (e.g., in the Beaufort Sea) effects; stripping of unrestorable lands often taken forcibly by eminent domain (e.g., in the Powder River basin); foreclosure of other land-uses; irretrievable damage to estuaries, tundra, seabed, and other fragile areas; boom-and-bust towns; serious and unavoidable hazards to workers; water shortages, especially for Western agriculture; massive pollution of watersheds and airsheds with combustion products, carcinogens from coal conversion, salts from shale conversion, and heavy metals; waste heat sufficient, by 2000, to warm the freshwater runoff of the continental United States (except for Alaska) by as much as 49°F; and destruction of the social and ecological fabric of whole regions.

Moreover, Project Independence implies an enormous coal burn. The long-term commitment to a continued fossil-fuel economy, with or without nuclear power, would therefore almost certainly produce at least a doubling of the world's atmospheric concentration of carbon dioxide. Major and perhaps irreversible changes in global climate could well result early in the next century.

THE NUCLEAR CONTROVERSY

One aspect of the Project Independence plan which raises formidable problems is the proposed massive reliance on nuclear fission through a multi-trillion-dollar investment. The required technical maturity, manageability, reliability, and economic viability of the technology have not yet been satisfactorily demonstrated. In fact, a searching examination of performance records and experimental results over the past few years leaves one shaken by the potential for disaster. Skepticism has grown among knowledgeable experts about the ability of unproven safety systems to prevent catastrophic accidents because of random failure or human malice. Threats and actual attacks on reactors and other nuclear facilities have occurred and are increasing.[4] Thousands of unexpected engineering failures, some of which narrowly avoided causing serious releases of radioactive materials (as in the Browns Ferry fire of March 1976[5]), have placed the quality of design, construction, maintenance, and adequate federal regulation in serious doubt. Despite the conceded need for meticulous technical care at every stage, it is ultimately the problems of human fallibility and malice that lie at the root of the nuclear debate.

Perpetual diligence is also required if the extremely large amounts of radioactive material generated by nuclear facilities are to be properly stored for the time needed to become safe. This could be up to hundreds of millions of years and one might well ask what human institution has ever lasted for the time required for safe disintegration of nuclear wastes.[6] Furthermore, in no U.S. nuclear-waste management program has the necessary diligence been evident in even the past thirty years. To cite a few examples: leaks in about a tenth of the Hanford storage tanks have released a half-million gallons of high-level wastes;[7] rain and groundwater have carried offsite in a few years radioactivity from low-level solid wastes that were not supposed to migrate more than a few inches in millennia. Biological research on the movement of actinides in food chains has yielded disquieting results. The problem of avoiding geological and social contingencies in waste storage remains unsolved and is not now known to be solvable.

Perhaps the most alarming hazard of widespread fission technology is its creation of materials which, in the hands of some individuals, could result in violent and coercive acts. The knowledge and tools needed to convert certain plentiful nuclear materials into a crude or sophisticated bomb, or into simpler weapons of mass destruction, are readily available.[8] In fact, tens of thousands of persons in the United States alone have the technical skills necessary to design a nuclear bomb based on information now available in unclassified literature. The nuclear materials, now created each year by the ton, may be created by the thousands of tons in a few more decades. They are already available[9] to those willing to take risks to acquire them. These include subnational groups, terrorists, criminal syndicates, perhaps individual lunatics, not only in the U.S. but in countries where the U.S. has continued to encourage and subsidize the importation of the necessary knowledge and equipment.[10] In some twenty years' time 20,000 bombs' worth of plutonium are proposed to be shipped annually as an item of commerce, yet the international community has never been able to control hijackings, bank robberies, or the black-market traffic in heroin, or to enforce any worldwide agreements. More effective safeguards than those used today may of course be developed, at an increasing political and social cost, but fully reliable safeguards are impossible in principle. On an international level, governments are free to divert civilian stocks of plutonium to military use (contrary to a widespread misconception that such use of reactor-grade plutonium is not technically feasible). Such diversions can be made undetectable in principle and probably unpreventable in practice, even if detected. It is hard to imagine any political arrangements that can adequately protect millions of bombs' worth of plutonium from misuse for the several hundred thousand years that this material persists, once generated.

The people in this country thus face incalculable environmental risks if such a nuclear power program proceeds further. But there are other considerations affecting everyone. First, for each environmental impact from nuclear power there is a corresponding political impact. For nuclear power to succeed, people must adjust to the demands of the technology rather than expecting technology to adjust to people. Even modestly effective safeguards will infringe upon or abrogate traditional civil liberties[11] through surveillance, infiltration, private armies, and extended police powers. Protecting the guardians of nuclear waste from social unrest, strikes, economic pressures, and wars implies a rigid and hierarchical social structure.[12] An ability to make political decisions about nuclear hazards is so difficult that governments are tempted to bypass the uncertainties of the democratic process[13] in favor of a secretive, elitist technocracy.[14] In short, the technical imperatives of nuclear power are incompatible with the political imperatives of a free society. Communist countries claim, perhaps correctly, that they do not consider this a serious domestic problem. However, civilian nuclear power in free countries might bring about the very kinds of political changes that their military nuclear deterrents were designed to prevent.

An alternative—and hypothetical—source of energy in the distant future is controlled nuclear fusion, which is included in the more speculative energy scenarios as an ultimate "safe," "clean," and "inexhaustible" substitute for fission and fossil-fuel energy sources. It is of course difficult to evaluate, decades in advance, the costs and impacts of a technology that does not yet exist even on paper. Although fusion technology if feasible would have one overwhelming advantage over fission breeder technology—the non-involvement of plutonium—it is likely to share every one of the other crippling disadvantages of nuclear power listed above. It is likely to be extraordinarily expensive in capital, materials, energy, and human skills. It is therefore even more likely than fission technology to pre-empt the resources of society and to foreclose other energy options. Its safety is far from obvious. Plutonium apart, the problems of radioactive leakage and waste disposal may dwarf those of fission technology. Fusion reactors will utilize large quantities of radioactive tritium, notoriously difficult to contain, and much of the energy will be produced in the form of high energy neutrons, which will make the entire reactor structures radioactive. Finally, first-generation fusion reactors will involve the consumption of lithium, a material whose supply is certainly not inexhaustible and could probably not sustain a large energy demand for long. For all these reasons, controlled nuclear fusion does not appear to be a valid, promising option for future energy supplies. We recommend that fusion research continue, but at low priority. (Almost too obvious to be worth pointing out is the one controlled nuclear-fusion reactor already available to us which is safe, clean, inexhaustible, and large enough to supply foreseeable energy demands—the sun.)

In sum, the proposed energy system for the United States, whether based on nuclear power or any other high technology such as synthetic fuels or fusion, does involve certain unavoidable consequences for society. Many of the following effects are interdependent:

- compulsory governmental diversion of scarce resources (capital, skills, labor, special sites, water, etc.) from other priorities into the energy sector;
- a need for a central authority (often federal) to impose big energy facilities and their perceived risks on people who want neither;
- a huge concentration of political and economic power;
- conflicts between central (often federal) authority and local autonomy in all energy matters;
- concentration of industry in and around major cities;
- corresponding concentration of political power, enabling urban people to obtain the benefits of the energy while inequitably allocating the associated social costs to politically weaker rural minorities, as has already happened in Wyoming, Appalachia, the Brooks Range in Alaska, and Navajo country;

- a tendency to make patterns of energy end-use conform to the needs of the source of supply rather than to people's needs;
- encouragement of horizontally integrated monopolies;
- isolation and alienation of energy users from the unaccountable elite who supply, price, and regulate the energy;
- imposition of paramilitary controls to discourage strikes and sabotage;
- commitment by the political authority to support the continued uses of the energy system regardless of any inherent faults, and hence to suppress dissent—or use social engineering to bypass dissent—even in case of major accidents or technical failures;
- reliance on a few adventurous high-technology devices whose technical and economic success is speculative;
- development of strong central bureaucracies and technical establishments that favor the technologies they develop and come to dominate decisions about their use;
- encouragement, directly or by example, of similar evolution abroad, through export of similar technologies, and maintenance abroad of historic inequities and power structures.

Finally, the huge commitments of money, skill, time, political consensus, and rapidly dwindling fluid fuels required by present federal planning would soon put other goals, such as pollution control or social equality, beyond reach. There would be insufficient resources or time left to develop the less tangible goals. The dangerous complexities and intractable problem of the present federal energy plan have led environmentalists to a belief that Project Independence (including its revisions and updates) is unworkable, uneconomic, unsafe, unreliable, and socially unacceptable. This plan is not only environmentally unsound, it is fundamentally bad strategy.

THE ENERGY BLUEPRINT

It appears possible to develop a markedly different policy which would give the United States (or other nations adopting it) ample and sustained supplies of energy but which would eliminate or greatly reduce the problems discussed above.[15] A few new problems, mainly institutional, would arise, but would be capable of solution in ways consistent with current social trends and ideals. Such a new policy is being discussed in the international energy community. In the past year it has received much convergent support from analysts of widely varying viewpoints.

This nation and the world recently passed a fork in the energy path. The present path leads further toward a centralized high-technology future, an unsustainable energy future which requires huge commitments of monetary capital and the remaining stocks of energy capital. The other path leads to a future based on dispersed-income energy sources and soft technologies with far less reliance on electricity. This alternative policy can be perceived by leaping ahead—perhaps by fifty years—to a sustainable society, then by working back toward the present. Thus this country would not proceed blindly with present policy until the realization came, several decades and most of the energy stocks later, that it was too late.

The alternative energy-policy path proposed is actually a core of common concepts, oriented not toward the supply of abstract economic services but toward the satisfaction of human needs. The key elements include conservation (at the end-use, but especially within the energy industry itself), matching energy quality to end-use requirements (to avoid enormous conversion losses), capital conservation, rapid development and utilization of non-electric solar technologies, and judicious use of fossil fuels through "bridging technologies" discussed below.

Consider first the matter of conservation. Recent analysis suggests that U.S. end-use efficiency can probably be doubled by about the turn of the century, through purely technical measures that are now available, economical, independent of lifestyles, and have been proven in several nations of Western Europe. Over the first few decades of the twenty-first century present efficiency could be approximately redoubled.

There is overwhelming evidence that improvements in efficiency would not only conserve scarce fossil fuels and avoid the side-effects of extracting and using them, but also save vast amounts of money for final consumers, increase national security and competitiveness, protect personal freedom of choice, and increase secure employment based on currently available skills. Conservation and prudent use of resources mean not loss but rather preservation of the "good life." The broader question of what we want our society to be and how much energy its tasks require asks just how much energy is appropriate and how far inanimate energy is to substitute for human labor. Humanity and humane values may be less endangered by too little energy than by too much when it is unaccompanied by self-discipline.[16] Our basic recommendations therefore are:

- **To avoid the formidable economic and political costs of further centralized electrification, we should make every effort to supply energy only in the quality needed for the task at hand and not to use up quality electricity or premium fuels for unnecessary purposes.**

Study of energy end-uses has revealed that more than half of delivered energy in the United States (generally more abroad) is required as heat, mainly at low and moderate temperatures, and that only a small fraction of end-uses can use to advantage the versatility and high energy quality of electricity. It appears that the United States, like other industrial countries, already has far

The Energy Economy

more electricity than it can thermodynamically justify. Reducing electricity generation would save enormous amounts of capital and fuel by decreasing the wastes associated with central power stations. It would emphasize district heating and the cogeneration of electricity in factories as a byproduct of existing process steam. It would develop technologies that supply low-temperature heating and cooling directly, and phase out the use of high-flame temperatures (especially from natural gas) for spaceheating. It would encourage industry to capture waste heat. To aid in this task the following is recommended:

- **The prompt development by the Energy Research and Development Administration (ERDA) of an inventory of energy end-uses by quality needs, geographical clustering, and unit scale**—a data base that, astonishingly, does not now appear to exist anywhere.

Conservation, especially by matching energy supply in *quality* to end-use needs, constitutes half of the change of direction. The other half is to match *scale* to needs. We now distribute energy from complex central sources, each large enough to run a sizable city. But evidence is emerging[17] that small systems situated near the point of use can be cheaper than large systems.

- **Smaller-scale energy generation systems should be developed and promoted.**

Small systems near the point of use, in single buildings or in neighborhoods, bring the advantages of technical simplicity, reduce distribution costs, and allow for small or no distribution losses. A small system means low administrative overheads; it offers resistance to monopoly practices and a low risk of technical failure or of mistimed demand forecasts. It reduces the financial burdens of interest and its escalation during lengthy construction. It greatly simplifies storage problems, makes modification and repair easier. It lessens the chance of large-scale failure which in large systems requires costly backup

capacity, such as "spinning reserve" on electrical grids.
- **We recommend a rapid move from dependence on depletable energy capital to renewable energy income.**

This would require a diverse range of relatively simple (though sophisticated) energy technologies that convert sun, wind, organic materials—even geothermal heat—to useful forms at a scale and quality appropriate to end-use needs. Rapid recent progress may make it possible over the next twenty-five years for the United States to construct an energy economy almost wholly reliant on these proven, economically attractive "soft" energy sources.
- **To buy the time needed for the transition directly to this energy-income the United States will need to build a bridge by using fossil fuels briefly and sparingly.**

With technologies designed specially for the transitional period, the United States could build at a scale that permits their infrastructure to be adapted later to other income-energy technologies. With a shift in emphasis to solar space heating and to converting organic wastes to fuel alcohols, coal can fill the sporadic gaps in our transitional fuel economy without doubling of the rate of coal mining. Furthermore this reliance on coal need last only a few decades, and can remain on a modest scale.

One more efficient technique for coal use is the fluidized-bed combustion process, which offers particular promise of rapid benefits without the need for massive research programs. European processes appear already to have achieved many of the aims of ERDA's long-term research program in this area.[18] Fluidized-bed combustors are particularly suited to cogeneration and combined cycles, district heating, industrial and institutional boiler backfits, and even packaged domestic boiler backfits. Moreover, new processes such as supercritical gas extraction, flash hydrogeneration, and flash pyrolysis may render obsolete our current approaches to coal conversion. In addition to the new processes, there are still some

The Energy Economy

old ones, such as low-BTU (water) gas, for local industrial use.

Many current economic calculations about energy technologies are misleading. Some people ask whether an alternative "soft" technology such as solar heat could ever compete with unrealistically priced fuels such as cheap natural gas. The question should be whether the alternative technology is cheaper than the conventional or proposed "hard" technologies which would *otherwise* have to be used in the long run to do the same thing. The answer is that soft energy technologies help to ensure wise long-term allocation of resources, and appear generally to be cheaper, even in initial capital cost, than conventional ones.[19] Of course they are financed differently—by single people or small groups rather than by giant institutions with special access to capital markets.

- **Non-subsidizing capital transfer schemes, of the sort now used by some utilities to finance roof insulation or water heaters, may be a good way to offer householders access to the capital they need to install soft-energy technologies.**

The small scale, technical simplicity, and engineering requirements of soft technologies allow for faster development and overall deployment than the large, high-technology devices on which present policy rests. They also offer better business investment with lower risk and quicker payback. Their use reduces risk of technical failure to almost zero. The environmental risks of soft technologies, designed with a modicum of care, are relatively small, tractable, and reversible. A recent ERDA-sponsored review[20] has confirmed that most of the potential adverse consequences usually raised as objections to solar technologies, for example, do not exist or are easily manageable.

How is the proposed policy advantageous for the average citizen? First, it avoids nearly all the political costs of present national policy. Whatever problems result carry with them far less coercion, disruption, and loss of traditional values than current policy permits. The social advantages are automatic and inherent: Soft energy technologies give users the benefits of their chosen energy systems, not a system selected by others. They would relieve dependence on vast control systems run by bureaucracies. They offer healthy diversity; encourage ecologically sound values and land use; are nonviolent, equitable, and nondepleting; take advantage of the free distribution of most natural energy flows; are ideal for developing countries; offer immense scope for local initiative and adaptation; are proof against inflation, cartels, and strikes; rely on consumer choice in many small refinements and additions rather than on centrally managed major projects; and offer the diversity, flexibility, and geographic dispersion to withstand surprises and resist disruption. Finally, and most importantly, many analysts now believe that if the U.S. promptly adopted such a soft energy policy and freely helped others to do the same, the result would be to virtually eliminate the main driving force behind nuclear weapons proliferation.

The advantages of soft energy are manifold and workable, yet all the proposals relating to it require much analysis, refinement, and debate. Environmentalists believe, however, that further work will only reinforce and justify their point of view. With one notable exception,[21] no federal study has even begun to address the sociopolitical issues raised here or dealt adequately with the environmental and economic issues.

THE POLICY CHALLENGE

Certainly many hard questions are yet to be answered in formulating national energy policy, but a realistic approach must begin with the recognition that, as a matter of economic and political fact, the current plan is a failure. The large coal-synthetics and oil-shale industries once envisioned will never be built because they waste too much energy and capital. Massive strip-mining of the arid West will never become publicly acceptable. The full exploitation of the Arctic is only a dream. The electric utility industry is faltering and may soon be financially moribund, in part because the utility laws force the utilities to be so wasteful of both capital and energy. And above all, nuclear power is dying. Dying not only because in economic terms it is too capital-intensive to be viable as a long-range energy option, but because the more debate surrounds it, the less viable it becomes as a political reality. Nuclear proponents are winning a few battles, but losing the war. Once these realities have been recognized, an orderly process of transition from the current obsolete plan must be initiated.

A viable energy policy requires much elaboration, but several critical considerations can be identified as priorities:

- **Intelligent coal technologies, both for direct combustion and for the local extraction of premium fluid fuels from coal before burning the remainder.**
- **Solar space-conditioning.**
- **A dispersed fuel-alcohol industry.**
- **Integration of solid waste, animal waste, and sewage management with energy and materials-recycling systems.**
- **Rejuvenation of urban mass transit and intercity railways.**
- **An overhaul of energy-intensive agricultural practices.**
- **All forms of end-use energy conservation.**
- **Maintenance of a fusion research program, but only at a low level, protecting a future option but without conviction at this time that it is promising.**

None of these measures will succeed if conceived as purely technical.

- **A more important element is to overcome institutional barriers, such as outmoded utility practices, mortgage regulations, and building codes.** These reforms will turn on public understanding of their importance, enhanced by a far wider, more sophisticated, and more wide-ranging discussion of energy options and goals.
- **Public participation, so far mainly formal, must become substantive and more wide-ranging.**
- **A progressively increasing gasoline tax, the proceeds of which are to be used to begin reducing the effects of automobiles.** This tax would have a significant impact on the poor, and thus other methods would have to be used simultaneously to attack the problems of poverty.
- **Discontinued expansion of the interstate highway system and diversion of the funds and attention to the nation's railroads.**
- **Maintenance of mandatory fuel-economy standards for automobiles and extension of them to other vehicles, including aircraft.**
- **Enforcement of the 55 mph speed limit through federal sanctions against nonparticipating states.**

Much of the initiative should and will continue to come from the local and state levels. However, true leadership from the federal establishment is also essential, not the one-sided, promotional rhetoric of the past. Executive branch pressure to adopt particular technologies must not substitute for honest exploration of a wide array of options in continuous dialogue with the lay public.

- **In the area of nuclear power a plan is needed for the orderly phasing-out over about ten years of existing facilities and the repeal of the Price-Anderson Act, which arbitrarily limits liability for reactor accidents.**

The phase-out must include a halt to exports of nulcear technology and knowledge (except for safety's sake) and of nuclear fuel, for which soft-energy systems would be substituted. The phase-out process would clearly terminate the fast-breeder program and all other steps toward a plutonium economy[22] (such as operation of the Barnwell reprocessing plant), which is now being urged by many arms-control experts on various grounds; also termination of all nuclear construction and commitments and the derating, for increased safety margins, of any reactors whose shutdown would cause serious dislocations.[23] At the same time the owners of such reactors would accept full responsibility and liability for their operation. There would be opportunity to retrain at public expense many nuclear technologists whose skills would be urgently needed for other tasks, while the skills of those few who are highly specialized would be used to design the terminal phase of the nuclear program. The best technical strategy for minimizing possible residual hazard after closing down the nuclear business has yet to be devised. Utilities holding obsolete nuclear facilities would be encouraged to write them off rapidly rather than take larger losses later. Incentives should be offered to convert the non-nuclear portion of existing power stations—most of the investment—to non-nuclear use.

- **Utility price structures must be overhauled to reflect both policy priorities and sound economic principles.**
- **Subsidies to nuclear (and other) energy industries must be withdrawn and antitrust and securities laws enforced** lest alternative energy sources be deprived of the benefits of competition and entrepreneurial vigor.

Most of the above recommendations are generic and common to both the general energy strategy and the particular tactical elements that make it up: freedom of information, due process, public participation, political and economic accountability, enforcement of legal mandates, application of sound economic principles, and mindfulness of the limitations of economics. Other more specific recommendations could of course be added (and the list will grow): coal-mining that is safe for workers, sparing of long-term land values, and nondestructive to ecological and other resources; the possible exploration for or extraction of oil and gas on the Outer Continental Shelf; short-term approaches to nuclear issues, including non-proliferation and arms control; full, unsubsidized energy prices; and a hundred more. Similar suggestions are being made every day in every forum open to the entire environmental movement.

It seemed critically important here to sketch an overall energy strategy that environmentalists believe their grandchildren could live with, one whose detailed implementation would be far less likely than the present plan to provoke conflict or calamity, and one whose principles a large and growing constituency of those concerned about the future could wholeheartedly support.

Natural Resources: Will They Last?

4

THE FLOW OF materials through society is one measure of overall economic activity; at the same time it is a symptom of an unresolved environmental dilemma. In an industrial society, minerals are extracted from the ground, refined, processed, fabricated into products, transported, used, and ultimately returned to the ground. Although all the processes in this flow constitute "economic activity" and are included in such economic indicators as Gross National Product, the materials actually contribute to human welfare only while they are in use as products. Thus, the rate of flow of materials into and out of the system is actually a measure of waste: the true measure of the contribution of materials to human welfare is the existing stock of useful products, together with the number of times they are used or re-used before they are ultimately discarded. Each wave in the flow, moreover, endangers the environment, by causing destruction of land in mines and dumps, pollution, noise, or the health hazards of toxic materials. These environmental costs have to be considered in calculating net economic benefits.

Of more long-term consequence, the materials flow means energy is consumed and materials are ultimately discarded in a state of higher entropy (or dilution) than in their original form. This increase in entropy is but one manifestation of the problem of resource depletion. The supply of low-entropy minerals is finite, and the time scale for depletion (established exploitable reserves divided by current rate of use) for many important metals is only a few decades. *Any* consumption of these limited materials is a real cost, in the sense that it limits the resource for the future and diminishes opportunities for generations to come—not to mention our own. This closing of options is the classic concern of environmentalists.

The traditional economic treatment of resource depletion is that the rising price of a dwindling material will promote the utilization of less rich or less accessible sources of supply and the introduction of substitute materials. Apart from the fact that some materials—such as helium and mercury—have unique properties and no foreseeable substitutes, both solutions usually involve a rise in the real costs (including social costs) of the materials, and an increase in energy expenditure.

For many decades the real prices of minerals remained more or less constant, despite the depletion of the richest sources of supply, as a result of technological improvements in extraction. But in the process the extraction and fabrication of minerals have become highly energy-intensive, so that the real prices of many minerals are now heavily dependent on the price of energy. Hence the broad problems of energy supply discussed in the previous chapter imply a correspondingly broad problem of materials availability. Environmentalists believe that most options for future energy supply will prove expensive in real terms, so it can be expected that most materials prices will rise in the future, while those of genuinely scarce materials will soar.

The industrialized world, whose prosperity has been built on abundant supplies of easily accessible energy and minerals, now appears to be approaching a period of materials scarcity. Although it is unlikely that supplies of individual materials will abruptly "run out" (except perhaps through a politically-motivated embargo or similar cartel action), we expect real prices of materials to rise progressively; this effectively makes the materials unavailable for use by society. The sooner that industrialized societies respond to the impending changes in availability, the less painful the transition will be. It is particularly important that the United States take the lead in such a response, both to set an example to other nations and to refute the accusation that it is the world's most profligate consumer of material resources.

- **The United States should adopt as a long-range goal the achievement of a "Conserver Society," in which materials are used and reused to maximum advantage with a minimum of resource depletion.**

THE ADVANTAGES OF RECYCLING

Such a program would involve resource conservation, recycling, re-use, increased durability of products, and long-term economic and social changes to minimize demand for materials in particularly short supply. Of course, rising prices will by themselves stimulate these developments, but there are a number of institutional and technological factors which now hinder them. Some of these are simple and direct, such as high freight rates for scrap materials; others are more complex, such as the tendency for technological products to contain mixtures of metals (copper in automobiles, for example), which are difficult and expensive to separate during recycling. The recycling industry itself is small, fragmented, and undercapitalized; it is also a polluting industry (in part a consequence of the complex mixtures which it has to handle).

In general, both short-range and long-range solutions

to these problems are made difficult by the fact that our economic system does not take into account the costs of recycling, disposal, or resource depletion when setting prices. These costs are now imposed on society as a whole as externalities, in the form of disposal costs, litter, pollution, and rising future prices. To resolve this difficulty, we recommend that:

- **Society adopt as a general principle that the sale price of manufactured products incorporate the costs of disposal or recycling, usually in the form of a refundable deposit.**

A prototype of this principle is the 1971 Oregon legislation requiring deposits on beverage containers. This legislation has been notably successful, not only in promoting recycling, but in abating litter problems and in maintaining local employment. It should serve as a model for uniform federal legislation.

- **The federal government should adopt uniform legislation promoting recycling of beverage containers by requiring a returnable deposit and by banning bi-metallic containers.**

There is no reason, however, why such legislation should be limited to beverage containers. Society could reap a similar net benefit if the same principle were applied to other manufactured products, including packaging materials, appliances, electronic equipment, vehicles, buildings—and even military weapons.

A particularly urgent task is the reclaiming of junked automobiles, which waste scarce materials, litter, and pollute with toxic metals and organic components. We recommend that:

- **Recycling of automobiles should be promoted by deposit-type legislation analogous to the "bottle bills."**

To be efficient, the deposits required on new automobiles would have to be sufficiently large to provide a strong incentive for reclamation, and should encourage the reclamation of certain materials (copper, cadmium, chromium, etc.) in such a way as to reduce problems of resource separation and pollution at the time of recycling.

Little or no thought is given at present in the design stage as to how a product is to be disposed of or recycled. This is one of the major problems in recycling. To encourage manufacturers to take disposal into account, we recommend:

- **That manufacturers be required to label all products with adequate disposal instructions. Such instructions should clearly note the presence of toxic substances that might be released as a result of incineration or land-fill burial. The disposal statement should require federal approval, and where significant environmental impacts are involved, National Environmental Policy Act (NEPA) should apply to the approval process.**

In addition, products should be constructed for maximum utility and ease of repair rather than for planned obsolescence. And for products that are not economical to repair beyond a certain point, ease of recycling needs to be considered in the design.

We recommend further that:

- **The development and modernization of the recycling industry should be aided by research and demonstration grants, and by incentives such as tax credits, low-interest loans, price guarantees, and preference for recycled materials in government procurement. Discrimination against recycled materials (in freight rates, etc.) should be eliminated or reversed.**

Although as a matter of principle subsidies to individual industries tend to distort the economy and lead to inefficient allocation of resources, we believe that this particular subsidy would be in the national interest, especially as it would tend to correct the distortions induced by past subsidies of extractive industries. It could reasonably be financed by a tax or tariff on virgin materials extracted domestically or imported.

THE ADVANTAGES OF RE-USE

Although recycling is an essential feature of the "Conserver Society," it nevertheless consumes energy and often causes severe pollution problems. A more important goal is to increase the effective life of manufactured products, i.e. to promote re-use rather than recycling. Providing effective rewards for the manufacture of durable products is difficult, because durability is difficult to measure in advance, and because the product lifetimes which are socially desirable are too long to be taken into account by many consumers. However, simple, immediate steps include the setting of mandatory minimum standards for durability, requirements for labeling of guaranteed and expected lifetime, provision of consumer information on lifetime costs, and in some cases testing by government agencies (analogous to existing tests for automobile fuel economy). Automobiles, again, should receive high-priority attention in this regard, because their notoriously rapid depreciation involves not only a large drain on the economy, but substantial costs in depleted resources and pollution. We recommend that:

- **Mandatory minimum standards should be set for durability and sustained performance of automobiles (including at least the engine and drive train); these should be backed by a federal testing and consumer information program.**

THE FUTURE OF MINERAL SUPPLIES AND OTHER MATERIALS

A number of specific materials deserve special attention because of their industrial importance and uncertain availability over the next several decades. The main exploitable stocks of some are located in countries with which the United States has uncertain political ties. A partial list of such minerals would include tungsten, antimony, manganese, nickel, chromium, vanadium, cobalt, and platinum (not to mention uranium and fossil fuels). Although geopolitical questions are not the primary concern of environmentalists, we are disturbed that many crucial materials are in the hands of such countries. Because the United States depends on imports of these materials to an even greater extent than on fossil fuels from abroad, we recommend that:

- **The United States review as a matter of urgency its dependence on foreign sources of materials critical to industry and defense, and take steps to reduce this dependence by promoting recycling of these materials, developing standby substitutes, building up strategic reserves and negotiating reciprocal trading arrangements (mutual dependence).**

We note in particular the dependence of several current systems for automobile emission control on overseas supplies of platinum and palladium; and we recommend that:

- **The automobile industry be encouraged to develop emission control systems that do not require catalysts made from imported materials.**

A second class of minerals of special concern are those whose distribution in the earth's crust is discontinuous, with isolated patches of rich ores rather sharply distinguished from a general distribution at much lower concentrations. The rich deposits of some of these are being depleted relatively rapidly, resulting in the prospect of abrupt and disruptive price increases in the coming decades. Examples include mercury, zinc, silver, tungsten, beryllium, niobium, and copper. As the noted geologist Thomas Lovering points out: "Where submarginal grades of such ores exist, they are likely to take the form of many scattered small deposits whose economic concentration would pose problems comparable to those that would be encountered in the capture of large volumes of rare and small organisms scattered through the forest or the sea. Resources like these, and they are many, threaten real and restrictive shortages in the future." [1]

We recommend that:

- **Special conservation and recycling efforts be instituted for materials such as mercury, silver, tungsten, beryllium, and niobium, for which stocks of medium-grade ores to support future technologies appear questionable.**

Niobium may be of central importance for the development of future non-energy-intensive technologies. With potential reserves of this and other materials (e.g., rare-earth elements) uncertain, it is essential that existing stocks and known reserves be safeguarded. We recommend that:

- **A searching review be made of the requirements for unusual materials critical to the development of new technologies likely to be important in the foreseeable future; and steps be taken to preserve adequate stocks of crucial materials or to prevent their dissipation.**

Helium has unique properties which make it essential for cryogenic technologies, undersea exploration, etc. and substitutes for helium may never be found. Although the United States still has substantial reserves of helium, they are being heedlessly dissipated by the burning of natural gas. Thus the options for future generations are narrowed still further. We recommend that:

- **A helium-conservation program be re-instituted to preserve adequate stocks for long-term future use.**

A current technological trend is to replace many materials whose prices are rising (metals, wood, fibers, etc.) with synthetic polymers and plastics. We question the wisdom and long-term sustainability of this practice, because plastics are now made largely from fossil fuels and the process is energy-intensive. Although carbon in itself is not in short supply, stocks of reduced carbon (coal and hydrocarbons) are limited and unlikely to be available at competitive prices for many decades. The importance of coal as a bridging fuel, combined with the high total social cost of extracting and using it, makes it undesirable as an important source of raw materials for an economy based on high-volume use of plastics. Extraction of carbon from carbonates or CO_2 would require large and probably prohibitive amounts of energy. The only other medium- and long-term sources of reduced carbon that seem feasible to support a plastic-based economy are recycling of used plastics and wood. However, if wood is to be viewed as a long-term source of raw materials, it makes more sense to use it directly than to convert it at great expense to plastics. Accordingly we recommend as medium-term programs that:

- **Research and development be applied to methods for recycling plastic products as an alternative to disposing of them by oxidation to CO_2.**
- **Continued development of wood processing be supported, with a view to eventual displacement of many plastics by products derived from wood.**

WATER: A SPECIAL RESOURCE PROBLEM

Problems of water pollution are intimately connected with those of water supply, since the surface and groundwaters in the United States that are used as a common property resource for disposing of wastes are also used for industry, agriculture, and domestic and recreational purposes. Excessive withdrawals of water from limited supplies can lead to depletion of river flows, lowering of groundwater tables, intrusion of salt, salinization of agricultural land, and pollution of groundwater, rivers, and estuaries. Already water supplies are acting as a limiting agent on development in the semi-arid West, where the rights to water (nominally belonging in some cases to Indian tribes) are being aggressively competed for by established farmers, expanding cities, and large projected energy facilities and ancillary industries. Water supplies are also critical in some parts of the East, such as Long Island and south Florida, where withdrawal of groundwater for expanding urban populations is causing both supply and water-quality problems, and is not replenishing the aquifer.

One more example of the interdependence of environmental problems has to do with water: Water pollution problems are made worse in natural waters by high temperatures, and yet plans for massive expansion of electric-power generation involve disposal of much of their waste heat into lakes and rivers. The whole water-supply problem is greatly compounded by continuing large water-engineering projects of the U.S. Army Corps of Engineers and the Bureau of Reclamation. All too often nowadays these are "pork-barrel" projects which diminish the overall resource (by enhancing evaporation from impoundments), destroy land, wildlife habitat, and recreational opportunities, while providing marginal or negative real net economic benefits. The federal government has for too long subsidized unwise, economically inefficient, and environmentally destructive water-engineering projects, which in turn have permitted and stimulated unwise settlement and development.

In view of the critical role of water supplies in determining patterns of settlement, land use, energy supply, and industrialization, especially in the western United States, it is urgent that present water policies be reevaluated in the light of present-day conditions. Even the National Water Commission, which reported in 1973, failed to anticipate adequately the importance of water as a limiting resource, a factor now emerging in the mid-1970s. Although many of the Commission's recommendations are still valid and need implementation, major new initiatives are needed. We therefore recommend that:

- A new national commission be established to re-evaluate the problems of water supply, water allocation, and waste-water disposal, and to prepare a national water plan with specific consideration of its implications for industrial and agricultural development, population distribution and environmental impact. Pending the preparation of such a plan, large-scale new commitments of water or inter-basin transfers should be suspended.
- The general principle be adopted that users of water should pay the full costs of providing the supply (including external costs and realistic interest charges on capital investment).
- Water be recycled and re-used wherever economically feasible.

As specific proposals to advance these general principles, we recommend that:

- The Bureau of Reclamation be abolished, and its ongoing construction projects suspended, pending their re-evaluation and incorporation into the National Water Plan.
- The Omnibus Rivers and Harbors Bill be replaced by a series of specific bills in which each proposed water construction project will be considered individually.
- Currently authorized projects of the Corps of Engineers be re-examined for costs and benefits, using a realistic value for the discount rate (and eliminating the "grandfather" clause which at present protects economically inefficient projects authorized long ago).
- Recharge of groundwater with the effluent from secondary sewage treatment plants be adopted as a general practice in areas where disposal elsewhere is leading to depletion of groundwater.
- Experiments be conducted with dual water systems

(and dual pricing) in urban areas where water is scarce (using secondarily treated sewage for outdoor uses and new or tertially-treated water for drinking).
- Indian claims to water rights (whether by treaty or otherwise) be examined carefully on a case by case basis and, where valid, be re-affirmed and given priority over other claims.
- Special commissions be established to study the water needs of river valleys such as the Sacramento-San Joaquin, Imperial Valley, Colorado, and Rio Grande, where withdrawal of water from the rivers upstream has led to slow flow and salinization in the lower valleys or deltas.
- Universal (individual unit) metering be established in order to cut down on waste through leakage and to encourage conservation.

Water and Air Pollution

5

THERE IS NO QUESTION that air and water pollution continue to pose serious problems for the health and welfare of the nation. Recognizing these dangers, the Congress, through the 1970 Clean Air Act Amendments and the 1972 Water Pollution Control Act Amendments, set ambitious goals and short deadlines for improvements. Now, after almost six years of efforts on air and almost four years of work on water, how successful have these bold statutory initiatives been? The answer in part is that no one really knows for sure.

AIR AND WATER POLLUTION REGULATION

Thanks to efforts by the Environmental Protection Agency (EPA) and the Council on Environmental Quality (CEQ), more objective data about environmental pollution are available now than ever before. Nevertheless, it is still not possible to get an accurate and precise picture of the *amount* of progress that has been made in controlling air and water pollution. Particularly within EPA, too much emphasis is still placed on crude and often misleading indicators of progress, such as the number of permits issued or the number of court cases prosecuted. The only valid measure of progress is the extent to which (taking into account uncontrollable factors, such as weather) the air and water are getting cleaner or dirtier. To collect such information, better monitoring systems are needed. In turn, the regulatory agencies, at both the federal and state levels, should rely on such information in their decision-making processes.

From the information that is available, federal efforts to control pollution have produced mixed results at best. Emissions of most of the air pollutants for which standards have been established have been reduced somewhat since 1970. Ambient levels of particulates and sulfur dioxide have also improved. But the air quality standards necessary to protect health had been achieved in only about one-third of the nation's air quality control regions by the mid-1975 statutory deadline. Washington D.C. had more pollution alerts than ever before, and Iowa had its first. Furthermore, in the words of CEQ, "It is becoming increasingly evident that the air pollutants upon which our standards and monitoring have been focusing do not represent all the important parameters of air quality. In some cases they may not even represent the most important or informative ones." [1]

With respect to water quality, there is simply not enough information to form a reasoned judgment about national progress. There is no question that water pollution has been significantly reduced in some places. EPA's first National Water Quality Inventory did show a general improvement in control of organic waste loads, coliform bacteria, and other pollutants from point sources. But the latest national index from the USGS National Stream Quality Accounting Network reported that only about 30 percent of the monitoring stations had water quality that could be rated "good" with respect to aquatic life protection. The latest CEQ assessment states that "... the problem of trace metals is widespread," that "most lakes studied in the Eastern states are suffering some degree of accelerated eutrophication,"[2] and that the problems of land runoff and of toxic organic chemicals in water are serious and have not been adequately dealt with. In water, as in air, the regulatory deadlines established by the legislation are not being met.

Better information would give a more rational basis for evaluating the existing regulatory framework. At the present time such evaluation must be based on scant data and a lot of deductive reasoning and preconceived ideas. It seems clear, however, that the regulatory structures established by the 1970 and 1972 acts need strengthening in order to accomplish the goals they set forth.

It should be recognized that some of the major problems with the air and water pollution control programs are not regulatory and would exist no matter what changes were made in the laws. Which air pollutants are the most important to regulate is basically a question that can only be answered by more research. How to control non-point sources of water pollution is a problem that has no easy answers regardless of the regulatory framework used. However, there are at least two major problems with the current regulatory approach that could potentially be remedied by legislative changes.

First, the detailed regulation and prescription of remedial measures for particular industries and plants put the government at a distinct strategic disadvantage. The regulated industry almost always has the information advantage over the regulating agency, and the result is weak enforcement and the risk that the pace and content of the enforcement program will be determined by those doing the polluting.

Second, the absence of incentives for polluters to comply with regulations almost guarantees that the regulations will be avoided as long as possible. The current regulatory approach tacitly encourages polluters to delay compliance, not to develop new control technologies, and to do as little pollution control as they can get away with.

The most commonly proposed solution to the deficiencies of the current regulatory approach is to move toward a system of effluent fees or charges. Such a system would, at least in theory, overcome the major deficiencies of the current regulatory approach. But it is always easy to make a theoretical solution look better than the current situation. Limited experience with effluent fees in other countries, notably the Netherlands, indicates that the information requirements on the government for establishing fees are much greater than was previously thought. Nonetheless, the deficiencies of the current system are sufficiently grave that effluent fees should be attempted in the United States.

An experiment with fees in a limited geographical area is unlikely to be implemented or to prove much if it is implemented (because of the opportunity for polluters to locate elsewhere to avoid the fees). Rather, it is recommended that:

- **The fee system be tried out nationwide for one type of pollutant, such as sulfur dioxide air pollution, or for one industry, such as paper. The fee system should not replace the present limits but rather supplement the regulatory requirements in a hybrid approach.**

Under such an approach there would be a regulatory ceiling on effluents or emissions which could not be exceeded under any circumstances. Effluents between zero and the ceiling would be charged or taxed at a given rate, and might serve to define the concept of zero discharge.

During 1977 Congress will be reviewing both the Federal Water Pollution Control Act and the Clean Air Amendments. Ill omens for this process have already become apparent. The National Commission on Water Quality, for example, has recommended:

(1) That the application of provisions requiring industrial polluters to use the "best available technology" be delayed for five to ten years.
(2) That exemptions and delays in meeting the Act's 1977 standards be allowed on a case-by-case basis.
(3) That the "no discharge" goal for 1985 be reworded in such a way as to destroy its effect.[3]

We recommend that:

- **The principle underlying the "no discharge" goal (namely that the nation's streams and waterways should not be used as sewers) be reaffirmed and defended against debilitating changes such as those suggested by the National Commission on Water Quality.**
- **Timetables for compliance not be delayed unless it can be demonstrated that they are in fact technically impossible to meet. In this unlikely case, delays should be no more than minimal, in contrast to those proposed by the National Commission on Water Quality.**
- **The Act be strengthened so that the provision on toxic wastes is made much more effective.** EPA has essentially defaulted on its mandate to regulate toxic water pollutants such as PCBs and mercury. Although a recent legal settlement between EPA and several environmental groups will now require the administration to set standards for sixty-five toxic pollutants, EPA's commitment is still not in keeping with the intent of the Act.
- **The Act be strengthened so that sanctions are applied to states and area-wide agencies which do not comply with the requirements of Section 208 of the Act, under which comprehensive plans and regulatory programs must be developed to abate water pollution from both point and non-point sources.** EPA must be encouraged to strengthen its commitment to the control of non-point source pollution through (1) greater emphasis on state control programs, (2) a stronger policy of sanc-

tions against offenders, and (3) increased funding for research and data gathering on the causes and effects of nonpoint source pollution.
- **The Act be strengthened so that EPA's enforcement authority is strengthened, especially with regard to federal facilities, many of which are failing to comply with the Act's requirements.**

It is further recommended that:
- **In EPA's sewage-treatment grant program, efforts be made to reduce funding of growth-inducing excess capacity and to give more consideration to the impact of sewage-treatment grants on growth and development.**
- **Sufficient funding be provided for underlying research needed for an effective program of toxic pollutant control.**
- **More emphasis be placed on non-discharging land-disposal and recycling systems and on alternative approaches to the whole question of sewage, including non-sewage disposal systems.**

Some further specifics:
- **Separation of industrial and domestic sewage.**
- **Secondary treatment of the first rush of storm sewage which after a summer's storm has *E. coli* concentrations as high as sanitary sewage. Regular street cleaning will also help this problem.**
- **Research into substitutes for chlorination. Research evidence has shown that the addition of chlorine to industrial wastes creates chlorinated hydrocarbons, many of which are carcinogens.**
- **Regulation of use of salt for deicing highways to control sodium levels in drinking water.**
- **Emphasis, in the examination of the sewage problem, on toxic pollutants in sewage and their consequent effect on the water they are discharged into.** These toxic pollutants include industrial chemicals, agricultural and feedlot runoff, and household pollutants. An ap-

propriate first step would be an EPA study in selected urban areas to determine what is being discharged and where it is coming from. A household inventory of substances discharged into sewers should be included.

The 1972 Amendments gave EPA unprecedented authority to enforce their provisions through administrative and judicial channels. EPA has not taken advantage of that authority to force compliance with the law. A recent GAO report cites a high non-compliance rate for various provisions of the water pollution laws[4] and even EPA's own reports shown a poor enforcement record. EPA often exercises its enforcement authority only when forced by citizen action in the courts, a right assured by the 1972 law.

It is recommended that:

- **Additional funding be made available for staffing and that EPA's commitment to enforcement be greatly strengthened.**

The 1970 amendments to the Clean Air Act established the legal framework to reduce harmful air pollution and protect human health by the mid-1970s. The law directed EPA to proceed in three steps: first, carry out basic research into the effects of air pollution; second, focus public understanding of the risks by setting official health standards; third, establish regulations as needed to bring pollution below levels documented to be unhealthy. EPA has faltered in these steps with the result that the goals for the mid-1970s have not been met.

As required, EPA immediately set national standards for six of the most harmful pollutants, thus initiating a five-year schedule for compliance. However, until a recent court decision forced action on airborne lead, EPA had refused to proceed further in establishing the standards which are urgently needed for numbers of toxic substances.

It is recommended that:

- **EPA immediately recommence the process of**

establishing national air quality goals for toxic pollutants; special priority be given to the fine particulate problem (micron size and smaller) which includes airborne lead, sulfates (to supplement SO_2 standards already in effect), the nitrate family, arsenic, organics, asbestos, etc.

Because of their small size, these extremely toxic and widespread particulate pollutants travel great distances from their point of emission. Since local and state authority to regulate existing pollution sources does not extend to regulation of sources outside their region even though those sources may by contributing significantly to deteriorated local air quality, some expansion of EPA's authority to regulate new pollution sources and these long-distance existing sources would be desirable.

Instead of building a basic research program on the health effects of air pollution, EPA has chosen to base its research on discrete pieces of information it needs for short-term regulatory purposes. This research has dealt largely with the economic effects of various pollution control technologies on individual industries rather than on the link between those industries' emissions and human health. Since it skips the step of openly defining the risk to health, neither the public nor industry can understand the potential benefit of industries' costs of pollution controls.

To compound this problem, the Office of Management and Budget has refused EPA's requests for a larger research budget and currently limits EPA's research budget to only one-fortieth of the cost of a single Trident submarine. The result is that both the public and industry are being deprived of information that is absolutely essential to intelligent decision-making and investment policy on pollution control.

It is recommended, therefore, that:

- **EPA's air pollution research budget be increased drastically to permit a comprehensive research pro-**

gram on the health effects of air pollution and an adequate monitoring network.

Further support is also needed for the coupling of municipal transportation plans to regional air pollution control efforts. At present, major public investments are being made without adequate planning, and the consequences will only compound the difficulty of the air pollution problems ahead. As EPA considers and approves regional transportation plans, a basic point must be kept in mind: A system built around the automobile as the primary means of transportation is energy- and land-consuming; its continued viability under scarce energy and land conditions must be questioned. In the past EPA has not used its air quality authority to assist in developing viable transportation plans for the future.

It is recommended that:

- **EPA, in cooperation with the Departments of Transportation and Housing and Urban Development, exercise its authority to press for transportation and land-use planning decisions that reflect energy and land supply realities as well as the nation's commitment to clean air.**

Some further specifics:

- **Much more reseach on combinations of air pollutants that are actually associated with adverse effects—sulfates, acid sulfates, fine particulates, NO_x-ozone.**
- **Revision of air quality criteria to include combinations of pollutants, for example SO_2 and particulates, oxidants, hydrocarbons, etc.**
- **Further support for development of an external combustion engine.**
- **Reaffirmation of our faltering commitment to the control of SO_2 emissions. Recognition of problems of acid sulfate aerosols, acid rain, etc., now requires management of regional sulfur oxide emissions, not ambient SO_2 concentrations.**

- **Extension of the air quality implementation plans to include domestic and non-point sources.**
- **Desulfurization of gasoline if sulfates from catalysts indeed prove to be a health problem.**

SLUDGE

One of the prime examples of environmental interdependence is that of solid waste produced from the treatment of polluted air and water. Sewage treatment produces sludge at a rate which will increase from 5 million tons per year to 9 million tons per year during the next decade. If the dumping of sludge into the ocean is controlled, which must be done, this implies enormous land disposal requirements. Also, the related problem of controlling industrial effluents produces a requirement for ponding and land disposal. Air pollution control also has land use requirements in that the flyash and dumping of sludge from scrubbers is projected to produce about 100 million tons per year of $CaSO_3$ and $CaSO_4$ wet slurry. The only conclusion one can come to is that pollution problems can be readily transferred from one medium to another, but not solved in the process.

Among these solid wastes sludge stands out both because of its significant volume and because of its potential utility as fertilizer. At present, 25 percent of the nation's sludge is applied to lands: 20 percent to croplands and 5 percent to other lands. The remainder goes to land fill (25 percent), ocean dumping (15 percent) and incineration (35 percent).

The costs of sewage treatment and sludge disposal are significant. Operating costs already run $400 million per year, and $12 billion in capital costs will be required to meet secondary treatment standards across the nation. Since 30 to 50 percent of the plant costs go for sludge disposal, significant savings would be available if the potential resource value of sludge could be realized.

The utility of sludge as a fertilizer is limited by its contamination by pathogens and heavy metals. Although the pathogens are substantially eliminated by storage, it is unlikely that sludge can be used to fertilize crops that are eaten raw. It could be used for other crops—timber, cotton, and lawn-sod, for example—if it were not for the problem of heavy metal contaminants.

The heavy metals, which are concentrated by biological treatment and can poison soils, come from three sources: industry, storm water and domestic waste water. The major source is industrial metal finishing plants. The prime concerns for plant toxicity are zinc, copper, and nickel, whereas the prime concerns for human health are cadmium and lead.

Since there are no inexpensive technologies for removing metals from sludge, this resource will go unused unless the sources of contamination can be eliminated. It is recommended, therefore, that:

- **The state and local governments be encouraged to isolate and eliminate gradually sources of metal contamination and to exploit the resource potential of sludge for fertilization of nonedible crops.**

The Hazards of Toxic Substances

6

THE WIDESPREAD environmental pollution, which is often viewed as an unfortunate but inevitable feature of modern industrial society, has recently acquired a still more ominous significance. The problems of contaminated air and water are no longer a matter of primarily aesthetic concern: Scientists now estimate that as much as 90 percent of all cancer is related to environmental factors.[1] Prominent on the list of causative agents are carcinogenic chemicals and other cancer-causing substances which are dispersed throughout the environment either deliberately—food and feed additives, pesticides, and industrial discharges—or inadvertently—a result, for example, of agricultural or urban runoff.

Cancer has become the number-two killer of Americans today; and at its current rate, cancer will develop in 25 percent of the U.S. population. While effective treatments or a cure for cancer continue to elude researchers despite massive expenditures of time and money,[2] it has become quite apparent that prevention of cancer by reducing exposures to environmental carcinogens is a realistic possibility as well as an urgent priority. If the environmental sources of cancer which are being identified every day can be reduced or eliminated, the trend of increasing incidence of cancer throughout the population[3] can be reversed and a major improvement in the nation's health thereby achieved.

Human exposure to carcinogenic agents in the environment is frequently involuntary and unavoidable: In addition to harmful chemicals which pervade much of our diet, not to speak of our drinking water and air, carcinogenic agents abound in the workplaces of many Americans. But voluntary exposures—especially smoking and high consumption of alcohol, beef, and drugs—top the list of factors implicated by epidemiologists studying the relationships between cancer and the environment.[4] Sunlight and natural radiation are also on their list.

Although the precise relationship between these various factors and the onset of cancer has not been ascertained, it is clear that many of the exposures associated with increased incidence of cancer are preventable. Prohibitions on the use of carcinogenic food and animal-feed additives such as Red Dye No. 2 and DES, effective restrictions on industrial air and water pollution, regulation of persistent pesticides, and a coordinated program of pre-market screening of new chemicals to catch such harmful compounds as vinyl chloride, arsenic, and kepone, *before* their irreversible damage has been done, would go a long way toward achieving cancer prevention.

In addition to their impact as a cause of cancer, toxic substances produce a broad range of other adverse effects; these include mutation, birth defects, reproductive failure, central nervous system damage, and general lowering of resistance to disease. Low-level exposures to toxic chemicals also have a significant effect on fish and wildlife, which means that all facets of the globe's delicate, interdependent ecosystem are being affected—possibly irretrievably.

EFFECTIVE REGULATION: STILL A POSSIBILITY?

A complex and overlapping assortment of federal and state laws and regulations has been enacted to deal with environmental pollution.[5] Authority to deal with the specific health-related problems and hazards posed by toxic chemicals in the environment, however, is fragmented among various federal departments, agencies, and commissions.[6] The result is the inadequate protection of the public from exposures to toxic substances.

PCBs are widely used industrial chemicals which in the last decade have been found to be both toxic and ubiquitous in the environment.[7] Primarily because of extensive and unregulated industrial waste discharges into water, PCBs have been detected in high concentrations in river-bottom sediments, fish, and other aquatic and animal species. They have also been found in food-packaging materials and foods of animal origin, especially freshwater fish, poultry, and dairy products. Because of their chemical properties—long persistence, mobility in the environment, and a propensity to concentrate in fatty tissue—PCBs accumulate to increasingly high levels as they pass up the food chain. As a result, they are now present at high and potentially hazardous levels in fish and other foods consumed by humans.

PCBs adversely affect the health of humans, and many aquatic and land species.[8] Moreover, there is recent evidence that PCBs are carcinogenic in laboratory animals and, therefore, presumptively carcinogenic in humans.[9]

Although the health and other environmental hazards posed by PCBs are now widely recognized, the extent of contamination is so great that reduction or elimination of the problem defies both regulators and technicians. For example, reduction of the "permissible" quantity of PCBs in foods to a safety level for the consumer may require the FDA to prohibit many items of food from being sold in interstate commerce. Such a step, taken in the past because of high levels of pesticide residues in certain freshwater fish, had a devastating impact on the hard pressed commercial fishing industry in the Great Lakes. A similar impact on the Hudson River fishery is anticipated as a result of action taken recently by the New York State Department of Environmental Conservation to prevent the sale of PCB-contaminated fish from the Hudson River. This contamination results from years of discharges by a General Electric plant. In an out-of-court settlement, G.E. recently agreed to contribute up to $4 million to help clean the river, but unfortunately such a cleanup is simply not possible at any price in the foreseeable future.

A parallel dilemma faces the EPA, which is presently attempting to regulate industrial-waste discharges containing PCBs. The scientific evidence demonstrating the toxicity of PCBs warrants a firm prohibition on all further discharges into water. Compliance with an absolute prohibition is, in fact, technologically feasible within the next two to three years—but the relevant statutory provisions require compliance with prescriptive regulations within only *one* year. EPA must either ignore the evidence and the potential risk to public health—and issue regulations which can be achieved within the statutory deadline—or implement regulations which may result in the closing of plants and concomitant economic dislocation. A third choice, and the one most often followed in similar circumstances, is not to regulate until ordered to do so by the courts.

Other obstacles to effective regulation of PCBs arise from the fact that, despite voluntary restrictions on the domestic manufacture of PCBs, importation of PCBs from abroad continues unabated. Even a complete prohibition on future discharges of PCBs into water or air pursuant to existing law would not prevent continued importation and consequent environmental pollution resulting from uses not covered by the air and water pollution control statutes.

THE TOXIC SUBSTANCES CONTROL ACT

After five years of debate, the Congress has eliminated many serious gaps in regulatory authority over toxic substances through enactment of a Toxic Substances Control Act (1976). The two principal features of the Act are: comprehensive authority to regulate exposures to toxic substances not presently covered by existing law (such as PCBs); and authority for the EPA to require testing of both existing and new chemicals to determine the nature of health and environmental effects and pre-market screening of new chemicals for adverse effects (such as carcinogenicity) *before* they can develop into major industrial materials which would be economically disruptive to ban.

FINANCIAL PRIORITIES

Even with the additional authority provided by the Toxic Substances Control Act, the problem of discovering and dealing with the chemical carcinogens and toxicants already present in the environment remains pressing and is not susceptible to simple solutions. The consistent pattern of association between long-term exposures to often minuscule quantities of toxic pollutants and the development of many types of cancer underscore the growing urgency for effective corrective and *preventive* action.

In keeping with this urgency a shift is needed from the current emphasis on financial support for biomedical research seeking a "cure" for cancer, to increased financing of epidemiological studies aimed at *preventing* cancer. As the Department of Health, Education and Welfare's Forward Plan for Health states:

The Hazards of Toxic Substances

In recent years it has become clear that only by preventing disease from occurring, rather than treating it late, can we hope to achieve any major improvement in the nation's health. [Heart disease, cancer and stroke] are caused by factors (e.g., the environment and individual behavior) that are not susceptible to direct medical solution.

... It is, therefore, a basic premise of the prevention strategy that much greater attention and resources must be directed at preventing the underlying causes of disease rather than at the disease itself—at controlling cigarette smoking, alcohol abuse, *and exposure to toxic chemicals in the environment* than at the diseases which they cause. [Italics added.][10]

The battle for recognition of the environmental origins of cancer and other diseases is beginning to be (but is far from) won; the effort to ferret out and eliminate those sources has hardly begun. We recommend the following action:

- **Reorganize for better coordination of the many federal agencies currently sharing portions of the responsibility for dealing with the hazards caused by toxic chemicals. Request pressure from the White House for conscientious, timely, and effective performance.**
- **Pay special attention to toxic emissions from the combustion of fossil fuels and from synthetic fuel plants. These materials include mercury, lead, cadmium, uranium, and cesium.**
- **Assure that EPA fully implements and enforces the Toxic Substances Control Act both for new chemicals and for those already in the environment.** This program should be given very high priority and full funding to permit rapid filling of the gaps left by lack of regulation in the past.
- **Give special research priority to filling gaps in scientific knowledge necessary for evaluating chemicals, including the study of structure-activity relationships, development of short-term tests for car-**

cinogenicity, risk estimators for teratogenesis and mutagenesis, and techniques in behavioral toxicology.
- Shift priorities in the National Cancer Plan from the search for a cure for cancer to prevention of cancer. The National Cancer Institute should be directed to expand both its epidemiological studies and its program for testing environmental chemicals and to complete and publish studies already undertaken. (NCI completed experimental work with kepone in 1973-74; prompt analysis and publication of the results might well have averted the kepone disaster of 1975.)
- Give urgently needed support to research on the effects of commercial chemicals on vital organs.
- Establish a national register of birth defects, to permit epidemiological studies to identify environmental teratogens.
- License laboratories conducting experimental toxicological studies and establish minimum standards for acceptable work.
- Initiate an all-out effort to eliminate the single most significant cause of human cancer—tobacco smoke. This effort will need to have several component programs including (1) education, (2) elimination of USDA tobacco programs, (3) phasing-out of tobacco farming, (4) an escalating health-threat tax on smoking tobacco, (5) a total ban on smoking tobacco advertising, and (6) a much stronger health warning on packages, printed in the largest letters used on the package.

Spaceship Earth: The Life-Support System

7

MOST OF THE foregoing sections of the Unfinished Agenda have been concerned with methods of maintaining human health, welfare, and productivity as the nation and the world move from an era of abundance into an era when the strains of crowding and resource scarcity begin to make themselves felt. But human health and welfare depend on much more than a supply of food, energy, materials, and places to dump the garbage. As passengers together on a little spaceship—Earth—we are engaged in expanding activities that are not only beginning to harm the economic system, but also beginning to strain the entire life-support system of the spaceship. Human civilization increasingly impinges on the health and welfare of other species, with whom it is bound together and on whom it depends probably in ways more fundamental than is known. The integrity of the entire ecosystem is the original and traditional concern of environmentalists, whose attention to the welfare of their own species has not in any way diminished their thought for the well-being of the other million or two species on earth.

Although preservation of the planet's life-support system is ultimately a global problem, the recommendations listed here begin with measures that the United States can take unilaterally to protect that part of the ecosystem within its own borders. This part of the Unfinished Agenda (like population and food, as well as others already discussed) is most easily and effectively undertaken by initially putting things in order at home. Accordingly, the acquisition and management of public lands and the regulation of private land use in this country will be discussed first, followed by suggestions for U.S. involvement in global ecosystem preservation.

PUBLIC LANDS IN THE UNITED STATES

North America, including the United States, has long been a model for the rest of the world in the maintenance of natural diversity. Despite extensive exploitation by early settlers, the various natural systems of the continent have been protected by a relatively low human population density, and by the remoteness and harsh environments of many of our unspoiled areas. In the last hundred years the U.S. has been able to preserve substantial areas of its natural landscape, but the situation has changed markedly in the last two decades. The increasing size, affluence, and mobility of the population, the increased power of modern technology to change the landscape, and the rapid proliferation of off-road vehicles, have suddenly threatened the natural heritage. National Parks, once the envy of the world, are overcrowded and in disarray. National Forests, set aside for multiple use, are now overexploited, and the last great stands of virgin timber are marked for destruction. The promises of the Wilderness Act remain in large part unfulfilled. Beaches are overcrowded, littered, and polluted. The great Western plains are targets of rapid exploitation. The extraordinary natural systems of Hawaii, with their unique endemic fauna and flora, are steadily dwindling. And the last frontier, Alaska, is being invaded by the frontiersmen with their unforgiving technologies.

Spaceship Earth: The Life-Support System

The United States has entered an era of scarcity: It is no longer a country of scattered settlements with an abundance of wild and undeveloped areas; it is a fully settled country with fragmented and decreasing natural habitats. More than 2 million acres each year are paved, mined, settled, or otherwise developed, with millions of adjacent acres affected indirectly. The American wilderness has shrunk to less than 5 percent of the country's total land area of some 2.3 billion acres.

This pressure on the nation's last wild areas is coming just when scientists are beginning to understand fully the dependence of man's agricultural and social systems upon the natural life-support system of the earth, and the importance of natural diversity in maintaining the integrity of this system. Protected natural areas serve such essential functions as maintenance of soil fertility, moderation of climate, stabilization of hydrological and perpetuation of biochemical cycles, accommodation and dissipation of flood waters, pollution absorption, and the provision of habitat for wild flora and fauna, whose gene banks are beyond price. Each species is a potential resource of great value, since each one is its own unique biochemical factory. Such unique attributes can instantly appreciate in the scale of perceived human values from useless to priceless. Penicillium fungus is but one striking example.

Many species serve economic purposes, for instance, in pollination, in nitrogen fixation, and in the control of agricultural pests. In addition, agricultural scientists now recognize that the only way to keep one step ahead of disease in domestic crop varieties is to preserve the genetic diversity of an entire species, including wild progenitors, so that by selection and interbreeding different strains it will be possible to generate new combinations with the characteristics needed to counteract new threats.

Ironically, the increased understanding of the value of natural areas comes at a time when a majority of Americans are located in urban areas where they experience only minimal contact with nature. Isolation from nature can lead to the dangerous illusion that man's industrial system develops independently of nature, or that human technology can solve the problems of the life-support system, even replace that system entirely. The dangers of these illusions must be recognized and actions taken quickly to maintain the natural environment before much more is lost.

It is recommended that the United States adopt as national policy:

- **The goal of maintaining the natural diversity of landscape, fauna, and flora to the greatest extent possible. In particular, efforts must be made to preserve a broad mosaic of native America,** including a representative selection of all types of landscape and land use: wilderness, national parks, multiple use areas, recreational areas, rangeland, agricultural lands, wetlands, and urban areas, as well as a representative selection of our historical, cultural, and architectural heritage. Ecological studies show that continuity of habitat is essential for the maintenance of diversity; consequently, **natural areas must be preserved throughout the country.**

Land Acquisition

Federal acquisition of natural areas for protection is possible under six preservation systems: the National Parks system, State Parks, the Wilderness Preservation system, the Wild and Scenic Rivers system, the National Wildlife Refuge system, and the Alaska Native Claims Settlement.

(1) The National Parks system was established just over a hundred years ago with the creation of Yellowstone National Park in 1872. The purpose of the system was to preserve natural areas of public lands regarded as unique for their scenery, historical significance, wildlife resources, and recreational potential. Since 1872, the park

system has grown to include 288 parks and monuments comprising about 31 million acres of land. Most of these park units are in the Western United States in vast, mountainous areas of dramatic beauty. The more gentle terrain of the central United States and the Eastern and Southern regions have not been as well represented in the park system. Recently, however, greater attention has been given to representing all characteristic American lands, and conservation groups are working to include such areas as the Tallgrass Prairie in Kansas and the Congaree Swamp in South Carolina. The densely populated urban and suburban areas of the country have few National Parks, but the establishment of the Golden Gate National Recreation Area in San Francisco, the Gateway National Recreation Area in New York, and the Cuyohaga Valley National Recreation Area near Cleveland is an encouraging sign of possible change.

Throughout the United States are other vast land areas of natural, historic, and recreational value that are suitable for inclusion in the National Parks system. Much of the land controlled by the Bureau of Land Management and the Forest Service falls in this category. These valuable expanses are not at present protected from destructive mineral explorations and development or from submarginal timbering and grazing operations. The wildlife and natural beauty of the lands are being destroyed.

- **Specific areas of the Bureau of Land Management and Forest Service lands should be identified, studied, and added to the National Parks system by an act of Congress.** These additions should be made keeping in mind the fact that an important purpose of the National Parks system is to represent all major American land types. Parks near urban centers should be created to absorb some of the overwhelming demand for recreational space.

(2) Local funds are not adequate to provide for the creation and maintenance of badly needed state and urban parks. Local taxpayers and authorities should certainly bear much of the responsibility for these parks, and in many states they do so. However, more funds are needed as well as leadership and guidance from federal authorities.

The principal source of funds for land acquisition by federal, state, and local parks is the Land and Water Conservation Fund. During 1976 Congress increased its $300 million ceiling to $600 million for 1978, and to $900 million for 1980 and each year thereafter to 1989. Of these amounts, up to 60 percent is available to states and localities. It is essential, however, that this potential aid be made a reality each year, in contrast to past federal practices of reducing appropriations. It is therefore recommended that:

- **Monies authorized under the Land and Water Conservation Fund be totally allocated and spent.**

State and urban parks, which are run by local authorities, could benefit greatly from the experience and advice of the National Parks Service. Greater coordination of efforts and cooperation between federal and local parks authorities would undoubtedly result in benefits for all of the nation's parks.

(3) The Wilderness Preservation system, established by an act of Congress in 1964, represents another means by which the nation protects its natural land resources. The primary purpose of the system is to insure that key tracts of our country's federal wildlands are set aside, both as a legacy for future generations and as sanctuaries in which natural processes can continue without human interference. Congress sanctioned this system "in order to assure that an increasing population, accompanied by expanding settlement and growing mechanization, does not occupy and modify all areas within the United States and its possessions."

According to the definition in the act: "A wilderness, in contrast with those areas where man and his own works dominate the landscape, is hereby recognized as an area where the earth and its community of life are untrammeled by man, where man himself is a visitor who does not remain."

With the creation of the Wilderness system, 9.3 million acres of undeveloped federal lands were designated as permanent wilderness. Certain other areas under the jurisdiction of the Secretary of Agriculture and the Secretary of the Interior were mandated for study over a ten-year period.

The Wilderness Act was an important beginning, but its potential is far from fulfilled. To date, only 5.6 million acres have been added to the system. Vast areas of public lands, including many millions of acres managed by the Bureau of Land Management and suitable for wilderness, have not been included, or even considered for the system. The U.S. Forest Service has inventoried nearly 1,500 roadless areas encompassing more than 50 million acres of possible wilderness, but from this inventory selected only 12.5 million acres for further study. Alaska has more than 125 million acres of potential Wilderness system land.

Opposition to wilderness preservation is endemic in extractive industries operating on public lands—notably timber and mining interests. The industry viewpoint on wilderness often weighs heavily in Congress, and frequently the more utilization-oriented federal agencies recommend minimal acreage for inclusion in the Wilderness system. In fact, however, the potential Wilderness system lands are generally not very valuable for commercial purposes, as might be expected, since the most rich and accessible timber stands and mining sites in the nation are already being utilized and are no longer wilderness. Timber stands in many potential wilderness areas are unproductive, suitable for commercial development only through government subsidy. Mineral deposits in commercial quantities and grades are slight, and even those areas which could provide marginal mining operations are usually more valuable for their wilderness resources: clean water, air, unique wildlife species, and primitive recreation.

- **Congress should act favorably on pending wilderness legislation** involving approximately 30 million acres in national forests, parks, and wildlife refuges. In so doing, the Congress should have the complete cooperation of the Departments of the Interior and Agriculture.
- **The Secretary of the Interior should forthrightly determine the real wilderness potential of the 450 million acres of land managed by the Bureau of Land Management,** and provide interim protection, as required by the Bureau of Land Management Organic Act of 1976, until Congress acts to include them in the Wilderness system.
- **The Secretary of Agriculture should re-evaluate the roadless areas inventoried by the Forest Service and promptly recommend to the President and to Congress those areas in their entirety which qualify for inclusion in the Wilderness Preservation system.**

(4) The act of Congress that established the National Wild and Scenic Rivers system in 1968 made it U.S. policy to protect in free-flowing condition selected rivers and their immediate environments for their remarkable scenic, recreational, geologic, fish and wildlife, historic, and cultural values. The act designated all or parts of eight rivers for immediate inclusion in the system and cited twenty-seven others for study and recommendation

Nineteen rivers have been added to the system, and reports on twenty-nine others are due by October 1979. For many of the rivers under study, this will be their last chance to be saved. Other highly scenic rivers not yet designated for study are jeopardized by projects of the

Bureau of Reclamation in the West and the Army Corps of Engineers throughout the country. A further danger lies in the rapid and incompatible development of shorelands.

- **With threats of dams, riverbank development, and pollution confronting many of the nation's finest remaining free-flowing rivers, the process of studying and designating them for wild and scenic river status must be accelerated, through full funding and the hiring of competent, trained staff.**

(5) Countless species have evolved since the beginning of time only to become extinct. Until recently, however, they disappeared as a result of slow-moving natural processes, as nature evolved yet another species to take their role or as they proved ill-adapted to the eventual changes in their environment. In recent times, by contrast, man's activities have destroyed habitats and species rapidly, long before natural processes could replace them. Within the last century, the United States has lost more than forty species of vertebrate animals and forty species of higher plants. At lower but equally important levels of the taxonomic scale the losses have no doubt been even greater.

Present attempts toward preserving biotic diversity are proving inadequate. The most significant efforts generally receive the least recognition and attention. Captive breeding programs and the reintroduction of species into habitats from which they have been extirpated are worthy, more often than not, but still last-ditch maneuvers. Such methods, even at their most successful, can work for only a small fraction of the biota. The only answer for the vast majority of species is habitat preservation and protection. The critical needs of these species can be met only through a comprehensive and carefully chosen system of reserves, dedicated to the management and perpetuation of their constituent natural elements.

The U.S. system of wildlife sanctuaries began in 1903 with Pelican Island in Florida. The National Wildlife

Refuge System Administrative Act of 1966 and the Endangered Species Act of 1973 reflected a growing concern for the preservation of biotic diversity. Today, there are 378 wildlife refuges which total 34 million acres. These refuges, and the legislation that supports them, represent a step in the right direction, but not a big enough step.

At this time, public-land agencies are reluctant to devote funds to studying the public lands for species, habitat, and migration route information. The Department of the Interior has been slow to expand the list of threatened and endangered species. Once a species has been entered on the list, the public-land agencies are often reluctant to alter existing programs to protect it fully. Instead, they usually proceed with existing plans, making token studies and taking minor "mitigating actions," while developing the land. The Bureau of Land Management and the Forest Service are slow to remove land from mineral entry or the timber-growing base just because of the presence of a rare plant or animal. The situation is particularly critical in the arid West, south Florida, and the Hawaiian Islands where entire ecosystems are endangered.

A major deficiency in existing programs to maintain endangered species is that they have focused narrowly upon maintenance of seriously endangered populations. This management design is akin to a health program which treats only the critically ill.

- **What is needed is the equivalent of a preventive-medicine program, in which the unit of management is the threatened ecosystem rather than the endangered species.**
- **It is essential that the provisions of the Endangered Species Act be better enforced. In addition, its scope should be expanded by legislative amendment to provide protection not only from federal action but also from private and other governmental actions.** The protected status of many species habitats and migra-

tion routes is being undermined by simultaneous use of the land for other purposes, the harmful effects of which are very subtle and slow to appear. It is important to enforce more strictly the requirement for environmental impact statements where species habitats are concerned. If existing legislation were fully implemented, wildlife management in the United States could be significantly improved.

- **More funding is needed for protection of both game animals and non-game wildlife.** In 1975 only 3.5 percent of all wildlife management funds and 25 percent of research funds from 13 federal agencies were devoted to non-game animals. Non-game species do often benefit from habitats protected for game animals, but the amount of funding is inadequate in both categories. Limited staff and funds are forcing environmentalists to select which species and ecosystems to save and which will have to be forfeited. Such priority decisions should not have to be made, for the U.S. has both the space and the resources to support all of its existing forms of life.

- **The existence of a central information source in the form of a resource data bank would be invaluable.** Professionals in the field still have too little information on many species and on questions such as the minimum requisite size of species habitats. The minimum land area to protect Alaskan ecosystems is but one example of such research priorities. In some cases privately or publicly sponsored inventories of states or regions can supply some of this information. In others, little data are available. The Nature Conservancy's State Natural Heritage Programs have been designed with these critical information needs in mind, and are currently accumulating information from widely scattered sources in a data bank. This data base should be centralized and made available to all those who recognize the necessity of preserving biotic diversity. If increased efforts to protect endangered species are to be successful, more and better data are needed to inform the efforts.

The international problem of endangered marine species (especially marine mammals) is especially depressing because it is so difficult to obtain the necessary international cooperation for effective protection. In addition a new threat to marine species is on the horizon. Since yet another heated and often bitter session of the United Nations Law of the Sea Conference adjourned without providing the international framework for legally mining the ocean floors, intense corporate pressure can be expected for unilateral action. Congress will probably be asked next year for legislation allowing the U.S. government to license deep seabed mining by American companies. What the mining companies want is a law that will give them some tangible guarantee that any eventual treaty will not force previously issued mining leases into a UN-sponsored enterprise. Deep seabed mining could be an ecological disaster unless strict safeguards and monitoring procedures are established first.

It is recommended that:
- **There be no deep seabed mining legislation unless it contains strict monitoring and safeguard provisions. Further, riches taken from the deep seabed should be heavily taxed and the revenue devoted to research, monitoring, and protection of ocean ecosystems.**

(6) Alaska is the last part of our nation to exhibit the vast ecological diversity that once existed across the entire continent. Its land forms range from Arctic tundra ponds and sweeping mountain valleys of the North Slope to the great river basins and endless uplands of the interior. There are delta marshes and coastal tundra in the west and grasslands, jewel-like lakes, and volcanoes in the southwest. Great mountains rise in the southcentral area. Rain-

Spaceship Earth: The Life-Support System

forests, winding waterways, dense timber, and immense glaciers form the southeastern panhandle.

The Alaskan wilderness provides habitat for a wealth of wildlife, some of which is endangered and much of which depends on wilderness conditions for survival. Mammal species of interest include the caribou, Alaskan brown bear, Dall sheep, moose, wolf, walrus, seal, and sea otter. In addition, migratory birds from all parts of the world nest in Alaska.

Fish and wildlife abound, but the balance of survival is delicate. Tens of thousands of caribou sweep over hundreds of miles in their migrational surges. Yet decades are needed to add one inch of growth to the filmy lichens on which they depend for survival. A single grizzly bear roams over a one-hundred-square-mile area to sustain itself. Thousands of wolves stake large territories and stalk their prey.

Alaska's delicate wilderness and heritage are under dire threat. Pressure to exploit natural resources for short-term profit is already having momentous impact on the Alaskan landscape. Corporate interests are rushing to obtain and exploit Alaskan oil, natural gas, minerals, and timber. The 800-mile-long oil pipeline breaching the arctic wilderness is nearing completion. A huge gas pipeline project is being planned. Logging, mining, roadbuilding, offshore oil drilling proposals, and urban development are exerting mounting time pressure on wilderness preservation efforts. If development is not to overwhelm and forever despoil the vulnerable Alaskan environment, Congress must take immediate protective steps.

The framework for the preservation of outstanding Alaskan lands was established with the passage of the Alaskan Native Claims Settlement Act in 1971. Of Alaska's 375 million acres, the federal government retained title to approximately 225 million acres. Alaska's natives settled their aboriginal claims for some 43 million acres.

The State of Alaska retained the right to select over 104 million acres as authorized by the Alaska Statehood Act of 1958, and has been granted 45 million acres of oil-rich tidal and submerged lands.

Congress took a beginning step toward lasting protection for Alaska's wildland heritage with section 17(d)(2) of the Native Claims Act. This section authorized the *temporary* withdrawal from development of up to 80 million acres "of federal national interest lands" (referred to as d-2 lands) to be studied for future inclusion in the National Parks, National Wildlife Refuge, National Forest, and National Wild and Scenic River systems. In 1973 the Interior Department recommended that 83.3 million acres be included in these four land systems. To date Congress has done nothing. Not one acre of the still unprotected, nationally significant public land in Alaska has been given permanent protection, although by law Congress *must* act by the end of 1978 when the current temporary protection will expire.

Many environmentalists feel the Interior Department's proposals to protect only 83 million acres of federal wildlands are inadequate, because protection would not extend to complete ecosystems. With this concern in mind, numbers of environmentalists have joined together in sponsoring a proposal designed, wherever possible, to preserve complete ecosystems in Alaska. A bill supporting this principle is now pending in Congress. It would set aside some 106 million acres (less than one-third of Alaska's land area) for inclusion in the four public lands systems.

- **Congress should be encouraged to act in 1977 on the proposal to protect 106 million key acres of Alaska's wildlands, through the creation of new national parks, wildlife refuges, and wild and scenic river systems.**
- **Whatever further development takes place in Alaska,**

it should be carried out in a way that interferes as little as possible with the way of life of native peoples throughout Alaska.

Land Management

Acquisition of public lands under any of the six systems just described is a necessary but not sufficient condition for public preservation of natural areas. Once acquired, these lands must be properly managed. If the current budget for public land management is compared with the size of the investment this country has already made in public lands, it becomes obvious that the management of these great resources is not being taken very seriously. No private company interested in staying in business would devote so little to the maintenance of its capital assets.

National Parks are seriously understaffed and underfunded. Congress has authorized only 8,700 permanent personnel to manage the entire National Parks system, yet the Office of Management and Budget has allowed the system to hire only 7,600. Congress has also added 34 new areas to the system since 1972 but, without new personnel to staff them, the Park Service has been forced to spread its ranks even more thinly. Americans are using the National Parks system more than ever before. Yet space per park visitor is decreasing as the establishment of new parks has not kept equal pace. Moreover, budget cuts have caused the Park Service to provide fewer amenities than ever before to the visitor.

- **The National Parks system should be funded at a significantly higher level so that it can hire the additional staff needed for the proper management of the park system.**

The concession policies of the park system have allowed, and even encouraged, excessive development and misuse of existing park lands. Under contract with the

Park Service, private commercial enterprises may provide visitor accommodations and facilities in the parks. In recent years, traditionally small, family owned concessions have been bought up by corporate conglomerates, the result being that concessioners often view the parks from the sole perspective of maximizing profit rather than providing the best visitor service and avoiding park resource depletion.

- **Concession policies must be re-evaluated and development limited.** Whenever possible, overnight accommodations and services should be provided outside park units.

Private transportation within the parks is creating serious problems of congestion and air pollution, even smog.

- **Plans are needed for an orderly phaseout of all private motor-vehicle transportation within the parks and for establishment of visitor facilities adjacent to but outside of the parks**

The Mining Law of 1872, still in force, allows almost unlimited private exploitation of public-domain land for mineral development, at the expense of all other resource values. The law has encouraged development of the most insignificant mineral resources, which are often mined in the cheapest possible way, without regard for water pollution or land reclamation. Most often, the renewable resources of the few precious wild lands are far more valuable in the long run than are those subsurface resources for which they are sacrificed. However, even land managers who recognize these values are helpless to prevent destructive development allowed by this archaic law.

- **The 1872 Mining Law should be drastically reformed or replaced with an environmentally enlightened law which no longer results in the wholesale abuse of the land, air, and water.**

The management of harvesting in the National Forests is in need of further attention. The Forest Service anticipates a doubling of demand for timber from the National Forests by the year 2000. Recreational use is also expected to double. Since there are at present 1.7 million acres of National Forest harvested annually, a doubling to more than 3 million acres per year will rapidly transform the National Forests to a state quite different from the present, with profound implications for all uses.

Although the National Forest Management Act of 1976 focuses on a number of problems that have long needed attention, important issues remain to be resolved. Ways must be found to transfer timber company demand to private forest land. Over 300 million acres of commercially attractive forest land is in private ownership compared to only 90 million acres in the National Forests. Yet the National Forests are drawn on to a much heavier extent. The special harvest programs for the Eastern National Forests are of immediate concern because of their smaller size as compared with the massive National Forests in the West.

PRIVATE LAND-USE REGULATION

Since far more land in the United States is owned privately than publicly, this land must be managed well, to protect the welfare of all species, including *Homo sapiens*. The costs of failure to plan the use of land can be high, whether they be measured in terms of destroyed ecosystems, unmet human needs, urban decay, suburban sprawl, or lost revenues. Unplanned land use can also be a drain on public funds; for instance, several billion dollars each year are spent to cope with the disastrous results of development in flood plains, while public investment in airports or in parks is often eroded by incompatible uses of adjacent lands. A rational planning process is needed to decide which kinds of uses should be encouraged on particular sites, and which should be discouraged. In this way, new housing for example could be constructed by reclaiming already developed land, or by utilizing site clusters, or by building on land where essential ecological functions will remain unimpaired.

Most land-use decisions have been made on the local level. Yet many localities, especially in rural areas, have been unable to deal effectively with the increasingly complex task of analyzing large developments, and protecting resources of greater-than-local significance. In response to this problem, several states—most notably Oregon, Vermont, Hawaii, California[coastal zone], New York [Adirondacks] and Wisconsin— have begun to reassert by legal means direct control over the limited number of land-use decisions whose effects have an impact beyond the local jurisdiction. They have also set minimum standards for local governments, to protect important resources, such as wetlands, aquifers, and watersheds.

These new laws are being upheld by the courts against claims that such land-use restraints amount to an unconstitutional appropriation of private property. The restraints are sustained as a valid exercise of police power, necessary to protect the public or the public interest from the harm which would otherwise result. A law, for example, which bars the filling of wetlands for development is sustained as necessary to prevent flooding, siltation of rivers, and interference with the marine food chain (the earliest links of which are forged in the wetlands).

Most states, however, have done little to exercise their authority over private land use. To a considerable degree this has been due to their protracted inability to acquire the federal funds which they have anticipated for many years, but not yet received due to the failure of Congress to pass a national land-use bill.

One such bill, sponsored by Senator Jackson and Congressman Udall in 1970, would have provided federal funds for states to identify and regulate development of their "areas of critical environmental concerns," and also to assure that local governments did not block "development of regional benefit." Jackson and Udall reasoned that land-use planning and regulation were best left to state and local governments, subject to certain federal standards of responsibility, and the sponsors of this bill acknowledged that it was intended largely to support reform of land-use laws in interested states.

It is clear that the nation's land-use problems will increase. Population has begun to grow sharply in smaller cities and rural areas, where governments are least able to cope with heavy development. The rate of household formation is exceeding population growth, because many more young people are starting their first household, while many more old people now live alone. The provision of low- and moderate-income housing will remain a problem for the next decade, and it will be a great challenge to allocate land to that necessary housing while minimizing environmental impact. The private market system alone is unlikely to produce the desired results.

The key environmental provisions of a federally funded land-use program would *require participating states to inventory, designate, and regulate areas of critical environmental concern. Such areas would include shorelands, ecosystems, key wildlife habitats and migration routes, historic sites, natural hazard areas, and renewable resource lands, such as aquifers and prime farmlands.*

In addition environmentalists recommend that national land-use planning legislation:
- **Protect lands adjacent to parks, historic landscapes and sites, small towns, and rural areas; and encourage careful urban restoration rather than the usual practive of demolition followed by skyscraper construction.**
- **Strengthen coastal zone protection, to include all barrier islands, marshes, estuaries, and shorelands.**
- **Provide for careful federal and state standards for**

management of the nation's privately owned forests, based on ecological principles of forestry.
- Preserve prime agricultural lands for farming purposes only, and provide extremely careful management of marginal agricultural lands to prevent erosion, fertilizer runoff, and spreading of pesticide residues.

THE U.S. ROLE IN PROTECTING THE GLOBAL ECOSYSTEM

Some of man's activities now take place on such a large scale that they are beginning to modify biogeochemical cycles and to change the physical or chemical bases of the global life-supporting system. All over the world forests are being cleared for fuel, lumber, and agriculture; productive wetlands are being drained; rivers are being dammed, straightened, or diverted; and natural vegetation is being cleared to make way for agriculture or industrial development. All too often the lands cleared for agricultural purposes are mismanaged, so that the fertility of the soil is reduced and land is lost to overgrazing, erosion, waterlogging, or salinization. In extreme cases, land misuse leads to local climatic changes and reversion of productive land to desert.

The destruction of natural ecosystems is particularly rapid in tropical lowlands, where both rain forests and savannah vegetation are being converted to agriculture at an unprecedented rate. Scientific studies have only recently demonstrated that the tropical rain forest, despite its legendary luxuriance, is actually a fragile and relatively unproductive environment. Its myriad species of plants and animals depend on each other in an extremely complex web of interdependencies; once it is cleared, the fertility of its soil is lost and the original forest system is almost impossible to restore. The minimum size of a unit of rain forest which will be sufficient for long-term self-maintenance is probably very large. Many biologists fear that the rapid clearance and fragmentation of the tropical rain forests will lead to their loss during the next few decades as functional ecosystems.

On another front, the effects of various pollutants on the ozone layer of the stratosphere are of special concern. The scientific community no longer disputes their occurrence, or their probable magnitude. Their significance is still a matter for study, but it seems clear that they will cause an increase in skin cancer and climatic changes. What is particularly disturbing is that the effects of the various pollutants are synergistic, so that even small amounts of each may not be tolerable if combined. The effects on the ozone layer take place on a long time scale; for the same reason the effects of remedial action will probably be delayed.

The United States cannot solve any of these problems single-handedly; it can provide leadership, especially since this country is one of the major sources of the materials and technologies that are threatening global ecosystems. Among the steps we might take on the international level are the following:

- **Action should be started now to phase out the use of fluorocarbon propellants as rapidly as possible. The use of alternatives to fluorocarbons as refrigerants should be encouraged and means to prevent leakage and to reclaim the fluids from scrapped units developed.**
- **Commercial SSTs should not be permitted to continue flights where the United States has jurisdiction, and the United States should use its influence to persuade other countries to phase out their use. Military flights in the stratosphere should be curtailed as completely as possible.**

- The United States should support studies of the future potential of overseas National Parks and Reserves for recreation, tourism, and research, with a view to advising foreign governments on rational development plans.
- The United States should support studies of the functioning of the tropical ecosystems, especially tropical forests, with a view to defining the minimum size of a self-sustaining tropical reserve.
- The United States should support studies of methods of restoring damaged ecosystems, especially tropical forests and islands.
- The United States should give increased attention to aiding reforestation in countries where forests have been seriously depleted.

Experience has shown that ecosystems on islands are particularly vulnerable to disturbance and exploitation, because of their isolation and evolutionary history.

- It is particularly urgent and important to preserve and restore the threatened ecosystems on U.S. islands. The most important are those on the Hawaiian Islands, which have more endangered species than any comparable area in the world. Special attention is also needed to prevent further losses on Puerto Rico, the Virgin Islands, the Aleutian Islands, Guam and other Pacific Territories.
- The United States should continue to exert its maximum influence to obtain a moratorium on whaling until scientific studies and international safeguards can establish safe limits and practices that will ensure the survival of marine mammals. Special attention must be given to the protection of porpoise populations from the ravages of yellow fin tuna fishing and to international agreements on deep-sea catches of food fish that will permit sustainable catches.

A LAND ETHIC

Ultimately the preservation of all the mysteries and wonders contained within the earth's ecosystems depends less on rules and regulations than on attitudes—the values of the one species that possesses the power to destroy or preserve itself and all others. The attitudes that led to exponential growth in the numbers of the human population must change. But even a stabilized human population could devastate the other species on earth unless values are systematically developed that curb such actions. Aldo Leopold called the necessary set of attitudes the "land ethic," and he carefully defined these attitudes and suggested how to attain them:

> All ethics . . . rest upon a single premise: that the individual is a member of a community of interdependent parts. His instincts prompt him to compete for his place in the community, but his ethics prompt him also to co-operate (perhaps in order that there may be a place to compete for). The land ethic simply enlarges the boundaries of the community to include soils, waters, plants, and animals, or collectively: the land.
>
> In short, a land ethic changes the role of *Homo sapiens* from conqueror of the land-community to plain member and citizen of it. It implies respect for his fellow-members, and also respect for the community as such.
>
> Perhaps the most serious obstacle impeding the evolution of a land ethic is the fact that our educational and economic system is headed away from, rather than toward, an intense consciousness of land. Your true modern is separated from the land by many middlemen, and by innumerable physical gadgets. He has no vital relation to it, to him it is the space between cities on which crops grow. . . . Almost equally serious as an obstacle to a land ethic is the attitude of the farmer for whom the land is still an adversary, or a taskmaster that keeps him in slavery.

One of the requisites for an ecological comprehension of land is an understanding of ecology. . . . The "key-log" which must be moved to release the evolutionary process for an ethic is simply this: quit thinking about decent land-use as solely an economic problem. *A thing is right when it tends to preserve the integrity, stability, and beauty of the biotic community. It is wrong when it tends otherwise.*

By and large, our present problem is one of attitudes and implements. We are remodeling the Alhambra with a steam-shovel, and we are proud of our yardage. We shall hardly relinquish the shovel, which after all has many good points, but we are in need of gentler and more objective criteria for its successful use.[1]

Although the kind of values Leopold called for have not yet been fully developed, tools are now within reach to remodel not just the Alhambra but the very species that inhabit the land. These are the tools of recombinant DNA genetic manipulation.

The New Biological Threat

8

THE ADVENT OF the recombinant DNA technique has brought biological research to a historical turning point no less profound than that reached by physics when the atom was first split.

The significance of this new technique is that it enables the scientist to create new forms of life (only bacteria and viruses at present) by cutting and splicing the genetic material so as to transfer gene-length segments of DNA from one organism to another.

Research biologists throughout the world are strongly interested in the technique because of what it promises to reveal about the basic mechanisms of life itself. Industrial and agricultural scientists are also keenly aware of the technique's possibilities. Production of pharmaceutical chemicals and the tailoring of crop plants are among the uses already envisaged.

The undoubted benefits of the technique for science and industry are matched by a unique and unprecedented degree of risk. The new organisms that will be created in laboratories throughout the world have probably never before occurred in evolution. Though every scientist can guess, none can say for certain what the result will be if these organisms escape into the environment.

THE HAZARDS OF RECOMBINANT DNA RESEARCH

The risks, it should be said, have been recognized and widely discussed within the scientific community.[1] In an act of self-denial that is somewhat unusual for a professional group, scientists have held a two-year moratorium and debate on the use of the technique. The moratorium came to a formal end on July 7, 1976, when the National Institutes of Health issued guidelines[2] prescribing the safety conditions under which experiments with recombinant DNA may proceed. The guidelines would prohibit experiments, such as 1) the transfer of DNA from certain pathogenic organisms to *Escherichia coli* (the normal bacterium of the human gut) for replication; 2) the deliberate formation of recombinant DNAs with genes for the biosynthesis of toxins or very highly toxic materials, such as botulism; 3) the transfer of drug-resistance traits to micro-organisms not known to acquire them naturally; 4) the deliberate creation of plant pathogens of recombinant DNA that are likely to increase virulence and host range. Experiments that are permitted are subject to various combinations of physical and biological containment.

The guidelines represent a serious effort to address the problem of risk, and one that has been widely commended as a farsighted and disinterested act of self-regulation by the scientific community. The guidelines are certainly commendable, but the crucial question remains, "Are they adequate?"

That depends, in part, on who is asking the question. Most biological researchers are not only eager to start work with the new technique, but are also reluctant to deny the ultimate beneficence of any new knowledge. For them, the opposing risks and benefits may come to a balance at a different point from that chosen by those who have no professional interest in doing the research. The present guidelines were drawn up by scientists, with very little effective input from the public, and most scientists consider that they are about as restrictive as they could be without constituting an unacceptable impediment to research.

Others may disagree, and for the following reasons.

First, the threat to the environment presented by the recombinant DNA technique is not that of any ordinary type of pollution. It is different because it is irreversible. When chemicals are found to be toxic, production can cease. When radiation escapes, it usually affects a limited area and in any case decays after a time. But new forms of life cannot be recalled from nature. Once successfully established, they may be company for all future generations of man.

At worst imagining, some form of life might be created that would be pathogenic for man or one of his domestic species. Suppose that, for reasons of medical research, a virus known to cause cancer in animals were endowed with the genes that enabled it to grow in *E. coli,* the bacterium that inhabits the human gut and nose. If the *E. coli* infected the laboratory workers and through them became diffused in the population at large, and if also the passenger virus were able to exert its cancerous effects in man, the stage would be set for a massive epidemic of human cancers. Such a scenario is not as farfetched as it might sound. It was a plan to conduct precisely this experiment that first set scientists thinking about the possible consequences of the technique.[3]

A human epidemic would be the worst possible consequence. Massive outbreaks of disease among a major crop species or major disturbance of a regional ecology could be equally disastrous for man.

Whether such accidents are likely to happen, no one

can say for certain. Many scientists believe that any laboratory-created organism is highly unlikely to find a suitable niche in nature. Others argue that all the possible combinations and reshufflings of genes have already occurred over the course of evolution. These are only guesses. So too is the idea proposed by Robert Sinsheimer of Cal Tech that there is a natural barrier to the exchange of genetic information between bacteria and the cells of higher forms of life.[4] According to the Sinsheimer theory, the barrier has arisen over the course of evolution as a basic way of protecting higher cells from bacteria. Many of the proposed experiments with recombinant DNA involve a deliberate breach of this postulated barrier.

The probability of creating harmful new organisms in the laboratory cannot be estimated, but the chances of such organisms escaping can be. Escape of some organisms from some laboratories is virtually certain. Even the most careful researchers become infected by the organisms they work with. In the Army's biological warfare laboratories at Fort Detrick, using the best available equipment at the time, there were 423 infections and 3 deaths over a period of 20 years.[5]

The guidelines issued by NIH specify in elaborate detail the physical and biological systems that must be used to contain the various categories of recombinant DNA experiment. But neither physical nor biological containment is as effective as a third kind—psychological containment. If laboratory workers really believe an organism is dangerous they will take the greatest care in handling it; if not, no amount of equipment will do the job instead. Many scientists do not believe that the work with recombinant DNA presents any hazard to themselves or others.

PROTECTION FOR HUMANITY AND THE ENVIRONMENT

The scientific community's approach to the issue, as reflected in the NIH guidelines, could be described as one of taking all reasonable precautions short of causing gross inconvenience to researchers. In a society that sets high value on research and the quest for new knowledge, such a course is not necessarily in conflict with the public will. But a course that put paramount emphasis on protecting human health and the environment would differ in the following ways:

(1) The effect of present procedure is to allow researchers to perform any experiment they wish (except the most obviously perilous), with the expectation that the answers to unresolved safety issues will somehow emerge. A more logical course would be to decide what safety problems need attention, and to concentrate the first round of experimentation on resolving them. If the problems were shown to be less serious than supposed, experiments could proceed with fewer restrictions than are at present required, and in the long run researchers would be better off. If on the other hand the problems were shown to be more serious than supposed, they could be addressed at the outset—before rather than after an accident occurs.

- **Decide which safety problems are of prime importance, then concentrate initial research on resolving them.**

(2) Industrial researchers are outside NIH jurisdiction and are currently not being regulated. Yet some large companies are already engaged in recombinant DNA experiments. One General Electric project concerns the production of bacterial cells which can efficiently degrade oil, and can therefore be used in cleaning up oil spills.[6] Im-

perial Chemicals Industries, Ltd., a major English chemical company, would like in the future to produce insulin and other chemicals by means of genetic engineering techniques.[7] And researchers at governmental agencies, such as the Department of Defense, are not legally subject to the NIH regulations.

- **Without question, all laboratory efforts involving genetic engineering techniques should be covered by the most comprehensive and complete guidelines.**

(3) A principal reason why NIH has permitted the use of *Escherichia coli* is that it fears the guidelines would be ignored altogether by the scientific community if this highly convenient organism were barred as a host. "You are . . . undoubtedly correct that *E. coli* is the wrong organism," wrote De Witt Stetten, NIH deputy director of science and chairman of the committee that drew up the guidelines. "Even at the Asilomar conference, however [where an international group of scientists first met to discuss the recombinant DNA problem], I detected little interest on the part of the majority to table *E. coli* and begin again from scratch with some other organism. The enormous quantity of information about *E. coli* appeared to dictate that, despite its hazards, this was still the organism of first choice. . . . I should expect that were we to make regulations banning activity in this or any other field of science for a number of years, we should find these regulations very difficult or impossible to enforce."[8]

The NIH guidelines, as it happens, are intended to embody the general principles laid down at the Asilomar conference, one of which is that, because of ignorance about the implications of the technique, it would be "wise to exercise the utmost caution." As the above quotation concedes, choice of *E. coli* is dictated by reasons other than exercise of the utmost caution.

- ***E. coli* should be prohibited as a host for recombinant**

The New Biological Threat

DNA molecules because of its known ability to inhabit not only man but also a wide variety of species and ecological niches in man's environment.

(4) Another Asilomar principle which has been lost sight of in the NIH guidelines is this: "It is strongly recommended that appropriate health surveillance of all personnel, including serological monitoring, be conducted periodically to establish a base for epidemiological analysis." The reason is obvious: Without health surveillance and epidemiological monitoring, there is no way, short of an accident, of checking whether or not the proposed containment measures are in fact containing.

- **Follow the "strongly recommended" principle of the Asilomar conference to monitor laboratories.**

(5) Recombinant DNA experiments may now be performed by anyone with access to a modern biological laboratory. Not all laboratories or researchers are of equal competence. The public would be better served if the use of the technique, at least in the early stages, were confined either to a handful of laboratories of unimpeachable reputation or to a single isolated site, such as the Fort Detrick laboratories. By and large, the scientists who have drawn up the NIH guidelines come from the best laboratories. The problem lies in coping with practices in the worst. Restriction, though foreign to the scientific ethos, is one obvious solution. And, at a minimum, adequate training courses are essential for all scientists involved with recombinant DNA. Of themselves, senior investigators might not ascertain that graduate students and laboratory technicians take necessary precautions.

- **Restrict recombinant DNA research to specific laboratories with excellent reputations.**
- **Provide adequate training courses for all personnel involved.**

(6) A number of experiments which the NIH guidelines allow should be restricted altogether until they are studied

further; for example, the introduction of viruses which cause cancer in any animal species into *E. coli* should be banned. Those with the cancer virus, SV 40, are permitted when the virus is "defective" (able to survive only under certain laboratory conditions). Since SV 40 can modify the genetic materials of human cells grown in laboratory culture and may be able to infect humans,[9] should experiments with this virus be sanctioned?

- **Restrict certain experiments altogether.**

(7) Accidental damage that might be caused by the technique is subject to debate, but there is no doubt that the technique could be used with devastating effect to cause deliberate harm. Offensive biological-warfare research was abandoned by the United States a few years before the recombinant DNA technique was developed, but its potential for these purposes, whether in crop destruction or human epidemics, may not remain unexploited indefinitely. Nor can the possibility of unilateral action by individual scientists be ignored. Sooner or later, someone may try to put the technique to malevolent use. But more to be feared is the do-gooder who believes he is acting for the benefit of mankind. For example: a scientist might decide he could save many lives by developing a set of viruses that would wipe out all known species of mosquitoes, with ecologically catastrophic results.

Nothing can prevent such deliberate misuses of the technique, but a code of ethics might raise some slight barrier to such actions.

- **Require all biologists conducting recombinant DNA experiments to sign a Hippocratic-type oath in which they undertook to do no harm.**

Enforcement of such a requirement would be easier than might be expected, if instituted at once. The preferred biological materials necessary for the experiments have been developed by a handful of scientists who are still the principal suppliers for their colleagues throughout the world. Adherence to such an oath could be made a condition of receiving supplies, or perhaps a condition for receiving federal research funds.

As a growing number of laboratories experiment with recombinant DNA, many questions remain unanswered. The NIH guidelines are a beginning: They have forced debate and restrained the use of a new technology. Further debate on additional restraints is now imperative.

Society and Decision-Making

9

THE PROCESSES BY WHICH U.S. society makes decisions about its environment have aggravated some problems, such as pollutants in our biosphere, chemical disruptive forces, the dissipation of natural resources, wilderness and wildlife, and the diminution of global life-support systems. What are these processes and how can they be made responsive to the environmental crisis?

The principal decision-making bodies are three. The first is the government, with its bureaucratic constraints and a time horizon limited largely to the period of accountability of elected officials—two, four, or, at most, six years. The second is the private sector, which also has a relatively short time horizon (determined largely by prevailing interest rates) and which, largely based on the operation of the market, responds primarily to return on the investment dollar. The third decision element is collectively the individual members of the public, informed by both government and the private sector, but employing a set of values (or bases for choice) that go beyond economic and political considerations.

NATIONAL PLANNING

A series of recent developments—double-digit inflation, 8 percent unemployment, an increase of foreign oil imports to 35 percent of total, to name but a few—has made it increasingly clear that all parts of the national socioeconomic system are not working harmoniously toward any well-understood goal. Since the warning signals of these problems were long apparent, it is evident that careful government planning could have forestalled much of the economic difficulty which faces this nation.[1]

The U.S. has surpassed the world in its development of planning techniques and has successfully implemented them in much of the private sector. For most Americans, planning is seen as a good thing when applied to business, to the local United Fund budget, or to the way other nations organize their affairs before they seek a loan. But planning is a bad word, and has even been called "immoral," when applied to the affairs of this nation.

The application of national planning to the complex interactive affairs of a great industrial nation arouses very real and legitimate fears of autocracy, mindless dictation, and the ultimate bureaucratic disaster—the possible end of democracy itself. Nevertheless, there is increasing national debate on the subject, possibly arising out of a growing fear that the institution of government is no longer effectively coping with the problems facing the nation.

While problems are clearly becoming ever more intertwined and long-term, our decision-making processes seem to continue to favor incremental "ad hocracy," or a bit-by-bit approach. An incremental "bit" decision on employment can trigger inflation. An incremental "bit" decision on phosphate detergents can commit us to tertiary sewage treatment, resulting in enormous capital demands and mountains of sludge impossible to use. The "bit" decision on fluorocarbons may have enormous and long-term implications for the ozone layer in the atmosphere. And so it goes on.

Public and private actions now have the potential for creating side effects which are, more often than not, sufficiently serious to require prompt correction. The real problem is that a reliable process is lacking whereby it is known in advance what the sum effect will be of any given combination of proposed actions.

This was also true in the past, but—because the pace of events was slower, timing was less critical, and areas of the country were less tightly connected—the implications of errors were less serious, perhaps more easily corrected.

Today, however, there is a real need for a better process of decision-making. Although incremental "ad hocracy" is highly responsive, it takes inadequate account of interconnections and side effects. And while central planning attempts to consider interreactions and side effects, it can be arbitrary and unresponsive to major economic and social forces. What are the alternatives?

If national planning is looked upon not as an iron pattern imposed upon society from the top, but as a necessary aid to decision-making, it can avoid some predictable errors without impinging upon essential freedoms. It can, in fact, lead to less duplication of effort and red tape in government and a more effectively functioning system of competitive enterprise.

The nation has always valued and maintained a mixed system of competition, cooperation, and restraint. What that mixture should be in the years ahead, however, and how it should be shifted in constructive response to new circumstances, will take more informed, thoughtful, and far-reaching judgment than has been demanded in the past. It will be necessary to secure better information and to understand more completely the trade-offs and interactions of available alternative policies. Most important, it will be necessary to give more attention to the long-term aspects of social problems.

The question of data is important. Many government agencies gather similar environmental data, which are all too often incompatible or in a form unsuitable for use and expensive to collect.[2] Therefore, we recommend that:

- **Efforts be made to simplify and improve the quality of all the data collected by the federal government.**

The biennial National Growth Reports series,[3] published by the Department of Housing and Urban Development through the Domestic Council, exemplifies the presentation of information needed for future planning.

Data alone are not sufficient. *A great deal of attention must be given to methods of analysis.* Too few people recognize the tremendous limitations of regression analysis as a means of forecasting. Much more attention needs to be given to the development of systems analysis techniques that emphasize feedback, causal structure, and delays.

Beyond matters of data and methodology, *much attention must also be given to the process through which planning will be carried out.* Two important considerations here are the goal of the planning process and the proper balance between accountability and independence.

Without a clarification of goals, planning could be a serious impediment to progress.

- **This nation does not need more efficient planning for further mindless growth in quantity; planning must stress an improvement in growth quality and address the location and timing of growth.**

The nation does need a consistent set of goals and objectives, based on the inherent ideas of the Declaration of Independence and the Constitution; however:

- **The preservation and enhancement of the environment need more attention than they were given by the Founding Fathers.**

In addition, there is a challenging need for a planning process which is sufficiently independent to allow it to address difficult and unpleasant problems, while at the same time maintaining a sufficient measure of accountability to avoid unrealistic separation from the mainstream of national thinking.

The most explicit model offered to date is the Balanced Growth and Economic Planning Act, which has been introduced into both the Senate and the House. If enacted, this bill would create a three-person economic planning board within the Executive Office of the President and provide encouragement to states to organize state-wide or regional planning offices as well. Members of the National Planning Board would be appointed by the President with the advice and consent of the Senate. Among other things, the Planning Board would prepare biennially a national economic plan and would coordinate the long-range planning activities of the departments and agencies of the government.

Environmentalists have many concerns about the proposed process, but two are of paramount significance. First, *national* planning is far too important to be seen strictly as a matter of *economic* planning to be left to economists. Second, placing the Planning Board within the Executive Office limits the time horizon of the Planning Board to the period of the President's accountability. The interconnected problems needing the nation's attention are long-term and cannot, therefore, be restricted to the relatively short time span of Presidential tenure.

Environmentalists see a need for better coordination of federal efforts to address the long-term national problems, including environmental concerns. Since the present proposal seems inadequate in several respects, it is recommended that:

- **A Presidential commission, including significant representation from active environmental organizations, be established promptly to investigate alternative ways and means through which a Planning Board can authoritatively raise long-term national** questions which might well be overlooked by the President or Congress.

The Planning Board will require a measure of independence from both the President and Congress. Its members should be appointed by the President, with the advice and consent of the Senate, to terms commensurate with the long-term nature of the problems to be studied, namely 25 years or longer. Funding should be provided from Congress on a rolling five-year commitment so that, at a minimum, there would be assured funding for an additional four-year period. Since the utility of the Planning Board would be severely reduced if it were unable to gain access to information, it should be given full subpoena powers, and the ability to enforce its subpoenas through the courts.

Two precedents exist for the kinds of tenure and quasi-independence suggested here. One is the Supreme Court, whose justices are appointed for life. The other is the Office of the Comptroller General of the General Accounting Office, a position of fifteen-year tenure.

But because independence without accountability is dangerous, the Planning Board should not be in a position to implement its plans and recommendations directly. Rather, it should be forced to argue its case before the public and its elected, accountable leadership and thus serve as an advocate for the long-term interests of present generations and generations yet unborn. In short:

- **Decision-making must be approached with more and better information, broader and more holistic analysis, and a longer-term perspective that corresponds with the fundamental problems now troubling the nation.**

An example of one such problem is the future of cities. The urgency of cohesive city planning has been most dramatically brought to the nation's attention through the fiscal plight of the city of New York. However, far from being isolated, this plight affects many other urban centers across the country. Until now, city planning, like the national economy, has been based on the assumption that physical growth is essential to prosperity. Cities compete with one another to see which can expand the fastest; and when city officials refer to "broadening the tax base," they mean that it will yield more taxes than it demands in services. The fact that yesterday's broader tax base did not solve the cities' financial problems does not reduce the optimism of planners concerning tomorrow's expansion, and any alternative to growth is thought to imply stagnation and decay.

Because the nation's population growth has slowed sufficiently to prevent cities from expanding rapidly in the future, some significant questions need to be asked and answered. How can cities remain healthy in the absence of population growth? How can redevelopment occur without an increase in density? Can vacant structures be economically renovated to provide attractive housing and stem the flow of people to the suburbs? How can jobs and homes be brought closer together to reduce transportation requirements? If the practice of razing buildings and rebuilding continues, where will all of the solid waste represented by present urban structures be put? Why should a city with more population and more problems than several major nations feel it must continue to grow in order to survive?

The answers to questions of this sort will require the development of convincing evidence that dynamic stability without decay *is* a possible and desirable alternative to growth. For this purpose, it is recommended that:

- **A major study be initiated by the Department of Housing and Urban Development, and supported by the National Science Foundation, to obtain the data necessary to assess urban growth and to study how the redevelopment of cities can be achieved in the absence of national population growth. It is further recom-**

mended that environmentalists be allowed to participate in the drafting of the study plan.

TECHNOLOGY CONTROL

Scientific discoveries and their application to technology profoundly affect the way in which a culture relates to its environment. The internal-combustion engine, nuclear energy, and nitrogen fertilizers (potentially influencing the ozone layer in the atmosphere) are but a few examples of how technology is derived from scientific knowledge in a way that fundamentally alters the human relationship with the environment. Positive and negative effects are possible in each case.

Society has evolved a number of processes for the control of the negative effects of technology. Technologists can be liable for injuries or damage. But the concept of liability provides only limited protection when very large numbers of people and large portions of the environment are endangered.

There are several "technology assessment" processes already being applied in society. Insurance rates are assessed on the basis of potential risks associated with the technologies used by the people covered in their policies. (One exception is the case of nuclear technology, where Congress has arbitrarily limited the liability because no insurance company would provide insurance at rates the utilities could afford.) The Food and Drug Administration assesses the potential implications for the health and welfare of patients before permitting the widespread distribution and use of new drugs. A similar process will now be needed for toxic substances being released into the environment in ever-growing numbers and quantities. And the Office of Technology Assessment in the Congress is studying the potential implications for some nascent technologies.

Nevertheless, society still has very limited controls over the application of technologies; the marketplace is the most influential factor. If money can be made from a new scientific discovery, it is generally applied, independent of other considerations. The technology for spray-paint containers, for example, offered convenience and profit, but by many estimates, the "unintended" applications of this technology in defaced property have created costs for society that far exceed the savings associated with the convenience of the intended uses. Similarly, decisions to develop the technologies for DDT, PCB's, Kepone and Mirex were made (and defended) largely on marketplace considerations rather than with thought to broader questions of human and ecological welfare.

The costs and the magnitude of the social threats are very large for some technologies. As demonstrated in a recent PBS Nova television program entitled "The Plutonium Connection," the promise of nuclear technology has given way to the threat of nuclear terrorism. The program documented how an undergraduate student at M.I.T. designed a nuclear explosive in a matter of weeks from unclassified information to be found in thousands of technical libraries around the world. The student could clearly have constructed the device from readily available materials, with the exception of the plutonium. A clever and determined person could steal or divert this.

Nerve gas provides another telling example. Not long ago both the U.S. and U.K. governments declassified and published the chemical formulas for the production of XV nerve gas. The necessary ingredients to produce lethal doses for millions of people can be obtained from most chemical suppliers for a very modest amount of money.

Perhaps the most critical dilemma in scientific inquiry yet to confront mankind relates to the recombinant DNA technique, which has brought biological research to a real turning point.

Thus technologies and fundamental scientific information have been developed with which single individuals could endanger large portions of civilization. In this situation liability is of limited utility since the damages incurred by the injured parties (if they survived or could even be identified) would far exceed anything that the guilty party could restore. It will be necessary, therefore, in the decade ahead to develop new controls not only over the application of technologies, but probably also over the availability of basic scientific knowledge.

Neither the basic nor even the applied knowledge about nuclear explosives could have been kept out of generally available literature without extraordinary changes in the structure of nuclear training and research, international scientific cooperation, and private industry. Reactors and bombs have so much in common that one cannot be the subject of collaborative civilian research—or of the public scrutiny that is essential for policy assessment—without the other also entering the public domain. To keep disassembly physics and equations of state from misuse, the world's research on fast reactor safety would have to be done under strict security. It might have been possible in practice, starting in 1945, to restrict *all* nuclear knowledge relevant to explosives by using pervasive military security, but then there could have been no academic or private-sector nuclear research, no training or even industrial participation of any consequence. That would have meant foregoing much of the personal and academic freedom and the political accountability that critics of fission technology fear its expansion may remove in the future.

The dilemma is profound: On the one hand, unbridled pursuit of scientific knowledge gives to individual scientists or laymen the power to terrorize or destroy large portions of the human race, causing enormous environmental damage that might persist for generations into the future;

on the other hand, efforts to control the development of knowledge are an inherent infringement upon the freedom of inquiry this nation has always valued so highly. There may well be a middle ground on which society can make informed judgments as to which forms of scientific inquiry are too dangerous to pursue, while preserving personal freedom through the vigorous exercise of its political institutions. A significant danger inherent in such a course, however, is that certain scientific inquiries, such as Mendel's genetics, might be ruled out because of their threat to the established order.

The recommendation offered therefore is that:
- **Whenever federal funding of new technologies is under consideration, the Council on Environmental Quality insist on environmental impact statements which go beyond the usual boundaries to consider the full sociological implications of the nascent technologies.**

A PRIORITY: ORGANIZING THE FEDERAL AGENCIES

In addition to planning and the management of technologies, a third concern of environmentalists involves the organization and priorities of federal agencies. At present the environment is regarded as merely a technical problem—a broken machine to be fixed—whereas in reality it involves social problems, and "technotwits" notwithstanding, social problems are not solved by technology. We suggest, then, that:
- **Environment be recognized as a top national social priority on an equal level with defense, employment, health, education, and commerce.**

This was the basic purpose of the National Environmental Policy Act, a purpose that has not yet fully been achieved. What is needed now is fresh leadership and a change of attitude.

Beyond this broad goal, there are other specific organizational changes that could be beneficial. Many suggestions have been offered as to how the federal government can be more effectively set up to deal with environmental problems, yet by itself government reorganization must not be seen as a panacea since it might well incur high costs and few benefits. Over the past few decades, the intended results of reorganization—improved agency performance and increased efficiency in the Executive branch—have generally not materialized.

There are two fundamental and interrelated reasons for these failures. The first is inadequate recognition of the basic determinants of agency behavior. The statutory framework, the congressional committee structure, and the agency's non-governmental constituency are more important determinants of an agency's processes and decisions than is its location in the Executive branch structure. Reorganization leaves these determinants unchanged and thus, not surprisingly, agency behavior does not change much either.

The second reason for failure has been the unrealized hope that creation of ever larger departments would encompass most of the programs affecting a particular substantive area. The impact statement process has demonstrated that virtually every non-environmental substantive area has potentially significant ties to the environment. Drawing everything together under an environment department would be no more workable than omitting environment from everything.

If the above analysis is correct, the creation of a single large conglomerate Department of Natural Resources would probably achieve not nearly as much as is hoped. All the various agencies included in such a new department would continue to operate autonomously as they have in the past because the statutes, the congressional committee structures, and the constituencies would not change. Such a department's necessarily greater number of bureaucratic layers would also result in lower agency morale and increased red tape. Most significantly, disputes between departmental components would be settled by negotiation within the department, thus allowing the Executive branch to appear more unified and easing the workload of the White House, the Office of Management and Budget, and other coordinating agencies. Because the disputes would not be visible to the public, however, there would be less citizen involvement in their resolution. Nor would they be visible to the White House, and thus there would be less opportunity for the administration to control agency policy.

Instead, the potential efficiency of the government should be examined in light of a broader and more gradual reorganization which would involve both the Executive branch and Congress at the same time. This restructuring would require appropriate changes and emendations in existing laws as well as substantial modification of the congressional committee structure. A larger number of smaller agencies could then be formed with a realistic appraisal of the influence of the statutes, the Congress, and constituencies.

INDUSTRY AS THE DECISION-MAKER

Although government agencies often seem rather remote and unaccountable, the private sector—industry—is far less accountable. Industrial decisions are informed largely by economic theory and respond primarily to return on the investor's dollar through the operation of the market. The effectiveness of the market's invisible hand in encouraging ingenuity and efficiency is certainly not to be discounted when it is working properly. Unfortunately, the market is imperfect in ways that significantly contribute to environmental problems—ways such as an exclusive concern with that which is "economic," an inadequate time horizon, and a reliance upon a flawed system of economic theory.

E. F. Schumacher has summarized the obsession with "economic": "In the current vocabulary of condemnation, there are few words as final and conclusive as the word 'uneconomic.' If an activity has been branded as uneconomic its right to exist is not merely questioned but energetically denied. . . . Call a thing immoral or ugly, soul-destroying or a degradation of many, a peril to the peace of the world or to the well-being of future generations; as long as you have not shown it to be 'uneconomic' you have not really questioned its right to exist, grow and prosper." [4] Aldo Leopold adds: "A system of conservation based solely on economic self-interest is hopelessly lopsided. It tends to ignore, and thus eventually to eliminate, many elements in the land community that lack commercial (economic) value, but that are . . . essential to its healthy function. It assumes that the economic parts of the biotic clock will function without the uneconomic parts . . . ," but they will not. [5]

The first point to make here is that environmental protection is clearly "economic." Without all of its parts working, the biotic clock, on which the whole economy ultimately rests, simply will not function. None of its essential parts can therefore be called uneconomic or even job-threatening. The Council on Environmental Quality has found that environmental protection has cost very few jobs. In fact, expenditures on environmental protection create new jobs and generate economic activity, and these expenditures in turn create vital services and amenities and provide real economic benefits. For example, a concerted effort to effect the much-needed rehabilitation of the nation's railroad beds not only would produce environmental benefits but also would promote the economic well-being of both industry and labor. Furthermore, labor can benefit from environmental measures because of associated improvements in occupational safety and health. Environmental protection, conservation, and the wise use of resources do not mean loss of the "good life" but rather the preservation of it.

But if environmental protection and conservation are not "uneconomic," why does the market not automatically safeguard the environment and scarce resources? There are more reasons than can be discussed here, but a partial list includes obstructions to operation of the market, an inability of the market to look far enough ahead, and some serious flaws in present economic theory. Consider first the obstructions to the operation of the market.

The necessary conditions for the effective operation of Adam Smith's theoretical "invisible hand" are often not found in practice in the many sectors of the U.S. economy. *A major challenge for the next decade will be to find means of using the market, including its imperfections, to induce environmentally beneficial behavior. In other words, ways must be found to curb economically profitable practices that are destructive to the environment, while still preserving the meritorious aspects of free enterprise.* As a start, we must stop subsidizing ecological nonsense. To this end it is recommended that:

- **The Council on Environmental Quality be given a sufficient budgetary increase to examine carefully environmental implications of the major federal subsidies now in effect.**

Special attention must be given to conflicting subsidies, such as those encouraging more insulation and those designed to keep energy costs unrealistically low. Subsidies in the form of tax breaks as well as federal payments must be considered. The government could save a great deal of money while benefiting the environment simply by eliminating environmentally destructive subsidies.

Also obstructing the efficient operation of the market are industrial giants, the economic equivalent of ecological monocultures. They distort the market through practices approaching monopoly, and, like a Midwest planted with a single strain of corn, do not contribute the economic stability offered by a larger number of smaller firms. We have witnessed the economic equivalent of corn blight in the cases of Boeing, Lockheed, and Penn Central. It is recommended, therefore, that:

- **Antitrust laws be vigorously enforced.**

Designed obsolescence is an industry practice that is facilitated by bigness and limited competition. The life-expectancy of many toys, for example, seems to be no more than 24 hours, and many appliances are designed with little thought to ease of maintenance and repair. Such practices facilitate a steady stream of sales, but unfortunately, as already noted, also increase resource consumption, contribute to solid waste, and reduce service jobs. To discourage these practices, the repair of damaged products and use of standard design and parts should be encouraged. It is recommended, therefore, that:

- **A program of legislation and economic sanctions, patterned after the French government initiative,[6] be initiated promptly against manufacturers who produce throw-away or unrepairable products, and who refuse to stock spare parts.**

A third factor working against environmental protection is that, at a 10 percent interest rate, the future value of forests and oil, among other resources, is discounted by 75 percent in only fourteen years. With the future so heavily discounted, the market cannot be expected to raise prices sufficiently and soon enough to prompt adequate conservation as scarcities develop. To correct this deficiency, it is recommended that:

- **Prices of increasingly scarce commodities be raised with an escalating tax.**

For example, natural gas, both intra- and inter-state, is

priced unreasonably low, but rather than passing on windfall profits to a few individuals,
- **An escalating tax on natural gas consumption is recommended.** The tax should increase annually so that after a five-year period the price of natural gas would correspond to the cost of producing energy of equal quality from income-energy sources. A similar tax should be applied to all fossil fuels and the proceeds used exclusively to encourage the development of income-energy technologies.

The economic theory of the market assumes no confusion about costs and benefits, but unfortunately confusion exists in the form of what economists now call externalities or external costs. Strip-mined coal, for example, is less expensive than it would be if the "external" costs of its production—the social disruption, the stream siltation, the gob pile avalanches, the flash floods, and the destruction of habitats—were included in its price. It is recommended, therefore, that:
- **To the fullest extent possible external costs be fully internalized—that is, reflected in the price of the resulting product or service.**

The flaws in the economic theory informing government and industry do not stop with externalities, but extend to our chief economic indicator, the Gross National Product (GNP)—an approximate measure of total goods and services produced annually. The GNP merely adds up the value estimate of some services (assets that are rented rather than purchased), plus the value of consumption (maintenance and replacement expenditures required to maintain the total capital stock intact), plus the value of current additions to capital stock (net investment). However, this computation is of little value when one considers that not all costs and benefits are included. Incredibly, those associated with natural service functions are excluded, but both consumption of resources and pollution of the environment contribute to the GNP. While research has been done on a variety of improved indicators of national progress, and continued effort in this area is warranted, the time has come when government must supplement the use of GNP and adopt improved indices of national growth. It is recommended that:

- **A Presidential commission be established immediately to recommend a more adequate indicator of the national economy and a new set of economic indicators be adopted. Further, it is recommended that environmentalists be well represented on the commission and that the commission's membership extend well beyond the ranks of academic economists.**

But beyond GNP, the whole theory of national economic growth is in need of rethinking. At present, research is focused primarily on "optimal growth rates" which balance unemployment against inflation. With population growth slowing and resource scarcities developing, serious thought must be given to the challenges of managing a steady state economy (SSE).

A steady state economy is defined by four characteristics: 1) a constant human population; 2) a constant population (or stock) of goods, including capital; 3) the levels at which the two populations are held constant sufficient for a good life and sustainable for a long future; 4) the rate of consumption of matter and energy by which the two stocks are maintained reduced to the lowest feasible level for the human population. Birth rates are equal to death rates at low levels so that life expectancy is high. For goods, it means that production equals depreciation at low levels so that goods are long-lasting, and depletion and pollution are kept low.

In a steady state economy, only two things are held constant: the stock of human population and the total stock of goods. Technology, information, wisdom, goodness, genetic characteristics, distribution of wealth and income, product mix, and so on, are *not* held constant.

Although a detailed understanding of a steady state economy is likely to be very important during the next decade, too few economists are yet working seriously in this area. We recommend that:

- **Research funds at the National Science Foundation and the Commerce Department be set aside and specifically earmarked for study of this field. Special attention should be given to: 1) further definition of the SSE concept; 2) the institutional adaptations that would be necessary to achieve an SSE; and 3) systemic, long-term models to study the complex problems of managing an SSE.**

Studies of the sort described above will require further developments for interdisciplinary research; the two disciplines that are most urgently in need of synthesis are those of economics and the physical sciences, especially thermodynamics. They represent two links in the areas of resources and energy which have not been sufficiently studied, nor are they well integrated into present economic theory.[7] *In the coming decade, the unification of these two fields, particularly as they relate to resource economics, will be a critically important research priority and is recommended as a funding priority.*

Research on energy efficiency, and environmental problems more broadly, is highlighting basic inadequacies in the tools of economic analysis. The time has passed when national policy can be based on simple projections of the past. Economic models contain grossly dubious assumptions and practices (including meaningless sums of unlike quantities) and are totally inadequate for the long-term projections now needed. Future models *must* therefore represent the causal structure, feedback, and delays at work in social, economic, biological, and physical systems.

EDUCATING THE PUBLIC

The research projects mentioned above will have to be emphasized during the coming decade if the necessary information is to be at hand for informed policy development. But efforts must be made to educate the public, or popular support will not be available for the difficult choices in the coming years. Curricular changes are urgently needed to emphasize ecological concepts, resource depletion, the effects of pollutants, human sexuality, and methods of fertility control.[8] Further federal encouragement and funding could accelerate developments in these areas.

The tendency of modern education to mold minds into narrow disciplines, in a way that inhibits holistic thinking, is considered by many to be a root cause of modern environmental problems. Scientific techniques stress specialization, reductionism, and the abstraction of unrealistically simplified concepts from the complexity of the real world. One preoccupied with the scientific method assumes—dangerously—that every effect has a cause. The hypotheses of science are based largely on this assumption, and the experiments that test these hypotheses are designed for a degree of isolation which insures that the assumption is approximately true. It is too often forgotten that in the absence of experimental isolation, real-world feedback makes causes indistinguishable from effects.

It is largely the neglect of holistic thinking which has led to environmental problems. By focusing its creative energy on narrow goals (e.g., increasing the GNP), the nation has made tremendous progress in some areas at the expense of others that now seem to be equally important. In the decades ahead, national objectives must be broadened to include, for example, healthy air and water.

Apart from formal training, our continuing education is through the media, especially television, and is shaped by the private sector in advertisements and programming. Television's impact on national thought and behavior is unquestionably pervasive. There are now more than 121 million TV sets in use in the United States in 68.5 million households.[9] Men, on the average, spend almost 4 hours per day watching television, and women spend nearly 5 hours, almost one-third of their non-sleeping lives.[10] By the time the average youth has graduated from high school today, he or she will have spent 18,000 hours watching television, more time than would be spent earning a bachelor's degree. During this time, the youth will have viewed countless examples that teach consumption as the answer to every need, and by the age of 14 will have watched 13,000 people being killed.[11]

Some television commercials seem to reflect an environmental concern. For example, many people remember the picture of the Indian with a tear running down his cheek. The message seemed positive: "Some people have a deep and abiding respect for the natural beauty that was once this country—and some people don't. People start pollution, people can stop it!" When one realizes, however, that this promotion was sponsored by a broad range of industries, many selling throwaway containers, an implied message may be seen: "Industry is not responsible for environmental litter; the blame lies with individual members of the public who start pollution and can stop it! Don't blame us for litter!"

Television's overall message has unmistakable environmental implications: namely, that we, the sponsors of these programs, can give you an identity, a sense of worth, and a solution to all your problems through the consumption of our products. Feeling a little insecure, depressed, lonely? The answer is some liquid refreshment in our convenient throwaway containers, a bright shiny new automobile that gets only 12 miles per gallon, some hair spray in a throwaway with fluorocarbon propellants, some deodorant. Whatever may be troubling your sense of worth or identity, the solution is not to be found in self-improvement, development, or determination, but rather in the consumption of more and more products requiring more and more resources and creating more and more waste and pollution.

If institutions of formal education were supported by advertising, school boards and PTAs would be outraged that children's teachers were pushed aside every 15 minutes with the remark, "Your teacher will be back in one moment after this message...." We feel similarly about libraries, schools, museums, churches, and national parks—those aspects of life which are associated with the development of the mind and spirit, with the socialization process.

Nonetheless, one of the principal mechanisms of contemporary socialization—the TV medium—is controlled almost entirely in the United States by merchandising interests. The decisions on what young minds will be exposed to, the role-models for their future adult behavior, have been largely turned over to the stranger in the box.

Recognizing the continuing influence of the television medium, environmentalists recommend that:

- **The Environmental Protection Agency, with support from the National Science Foundation, undertake to monitor and analyze the explicit and implicit environmental message contained in both the programming and commercials on television in the United States.** The analysis should document clearly what is being said about environmental issues, resource consumption, pollution, and lifestyles, and the implications for these concerns if the viewing audience follows the example set by the role-models on television.
- **The study described above with programming available on non-commercial systems and in countries like Sweden, or on mixed systems as in the United Kingdom.**
- **As a minimal step toward reducing the adverse**

environmental message of television while retaining the commercial system, commercials be clustered on the hour and half-hour to eliminate the need to design programs for the convenient promotion of products within the program itself.

Very clearly, television is a major influence on the American value system, the basic ideas that inform all actions and choices. This value system has enormous implications for the environment and is undergoing dramatic changes.

A Question of Values
10

AS MUST BE CLEAR by now, this book is about a world transition from abundance to scarcity, a transition that is already well underway. The growing scarcity of fossil fuels is only the most obvious of the symptoms. Everything is affected: land, water, air, resources, food, capital. Species and entire ecosystems—the essential sub-elements of the planet's life-support system—are threatened, and growing interdependence and uniformity among major units of human civilization continually reduce the chances that effects of local accidents and disturbances can be kept localized. But for better or worse, mutual dependencies between nations and peoples will continue to grow.

There can no longer be any doubt that the inhabitants of the earth share a common environment. As is made so strikingly clear in photographs from space, the earth's atmosphere is but a thin film no thicker on the scale of a twelve-inch globe than the paper on which these words are printed. Through fluorocarbon discharges, heavy combustion of coal, or perhaps even extensive use of nitrogen fertilizers, individual nations can take actions that will seriously alter this fragile atmosphere for other nations. These and similar interdependencies are unavoidable characteristics of life in a common environment; they have been eloquently described by Garrett Hardin in his classic article, "The Tragedy of the Commons." [1]

The essence of tragedy is simple enough. Imagine a lush mountain valley in which herdsmen live, free to graze their animals on the common pasture of the valley floor. In prosperity, the population of both herdsmen and cattle increases. As signs of overgrazing begin to appear, most herdsmen find themselves with at least one young animal that is not really needed. If the animal is slaughtered, the overgrazing is reduced by one animal, a benefit that is spread thinly over the entire herd and all the herdsmen. If the animal is retained, however, the profit from its eventual sale accrues entirely to its owner. The tragedy of the common pasture is that actions in the best interest of each and every individual are exactly the actions that destroy the commons for everyone.

The transition from abundance to scarcity in a commons requires a profound change of values. In abundance, personal interests and individualism are the keys to success and growth. In scarcity, the values necessary for survival are a paradox: It is in the best interest of each and every individual to put the interests of the whole society above his own; survival and stability are possible in no other way. Those who live in the common environment of the planet are now experiencing the transition from abundance to scarcity. The immediate challenge ahead is not physical limits to growth[2] (which are nevertheless very real) but the challenge of a major transformation in human values.[3]

Although both the transition and the transformation are global in nature, the United States has a unique responsibility in both cases. It is this nation, more than any other, that has enjoyed the economic benefits of a development path that is no longer possible for most. Yet many nations would still like to emulate the U.S. experience in exploiting the commons, and for every day that the transition proceeds without the transformation, the transition must ultimately become more painful and difficult.

- **There is therefore an urgent need for the United States to acknowledge its unique responsibility of leadership in both the transition and the transformation and to use its resources and knowledge to provide examples of how, in a "Conserver Society," quality of life can be preserved (and, for many, increased) even in an era of scarcity.**

One of the first items on the agenda will be a rethinking of the concept of growth. In a commons, survival requires a redirection from things that are merely countable toward things that really count.[4] Since many Americans believe only countable things really count, it will be necessary to reexamine the origins of our fundamental concepts of growth. The equation of growth with good[5] may stem from the way religious institutions have interpreted Genesis 1:28, which provides God's injunction: "Be fruitful and multiply, and fill the earth and subdue it; and have dominion over the fish of the sea and over the birds of the air and over every living thing that moves upon the earth."

Immediately after growth comes the question of equity. During the growth phase of life in the commons, it can be argued that growth will resolve inequity: If everyone's piece of the economic pie is growing, it doesn't matter that some pieces are much larger than others; everyone is doing better. But when the commons becomes overgrazed and growth slows, questions of equity must be answered with a different argument. Difficult as questions of equity are, the United States must take a leadership role in resolving them both at home and abroad.

Beyond these broad questions, there are a host of specific questions that need immediate examination. In the population area, for example, why do we as individuals want to have children? Is it selfish not to have children or to be parents? Are childless marriages wrong? Is a woman's place in the home? Only in the home? Why do we want the number of children we do? Do we have an obligation to future generations? Does a woman have complete control of her fertility? Should she? Is it selfish to want to have children of our own rather than to adopt and raise unwanted children? Should the nation increase or decrease its population? Should the poor from other nations be encouraged to come here for a better life? Do immigrants to the United States alleviate poor conditions in their own countries? Should the United States accept only well-trained technical people as immigrants?

Do we have an obligation, responsibility, or opportunity to feed starving peoples in other nations with our food? Should farmers produce food at a loss? Who is to pay for food that people cannot afford? Will feeding the undernourished temporarily reduce death rates and lead to inevitable disaster caused by high birth rates? Can birth rates be brought under control without development? Can starvation be avoided until development takes place? Is it wrong to be overweight while others starve? Are the resources available to make development possible? Should agricultural development precede other aspects of development? Should energy-intensive "Green Revolution" agriculture be encouraged? Could the peoples of the world (or even the United States) be fed without energy-intensive agriculture?

Is it politically possible to face realistically the energy crisis? Should 50 percent or more of our energy be spent in a highly electrified energy-future? Is the energy industry to become increasingly inefficient while at the same time raising prices and forcing conservation on consumers? Is it right to create toxic radioactive wastes that will require the supervision of a stable social order for hundreds of thousands of years? Do we express love for our children by poisoning their environment? What would we do with a cheap, inexhaustible, clean source of energy if we had one? Is there virtue in limiting the amount of energy available to a society, and at the same time the amount of mischief it can do?

Should products be designed as "throwaways"? What is a *disposable* product? How is it disposed of? Where does it go? Will future generations wish they had the resources that have gone into disposable products?

Why are our waterways and skies health threats to humans and other species? Is it too expensive to clean them up? What does it cost? Can we afford not to clean them up, especially when toxic substances are involved?

Have we had "dominion over every living thing that moves on the earth"? Can we do what we will with species and ecosystems? Have the benefits of services provided by the ecosystems been included in the economic calculus? How much is it worth to have New York's air blown out to sea? What would it cost to replace this service? Are the operations of ecosystems sufficiently understood to allow us to feel comfortable about creating new forms of life, even in highly protected laboratories?

What do our children need to know? Are parents teaching it to them? Are they learning it in schools? Are they learning it from commercial television? Are they learning something else from commercial television?

None of these questions is easily answered. In fact, a serious discussion of any one of them will almost certainly provoke heated reactions.[6] But it is with these and similar questions that the transformation must start. Where it will ultimately lead is still not clear, but a few indications are on the horizon.

One dimension to the question of environmental values can be ignored or discounted only at great risk—the aesthetic dimension. The spontaneous recognition by people of all cultures, ages, and conditions that there is a beauty in nature that does not exist in the man-made environment cannot be denied. Leopold sums it up well: "A thing is right when it tends to preserve the integrity, stability, and beauty of the biotic community. It is wrong when it tends otherwise." [7] That aesthetic response, which testifies however inarticulately to our quintessential connection with the rest of creation and eases our pain of estrangement from it, should weigh heavily in the balance when competing values come up for decision.

Beyond aesthetics and a deep appreciation of our ties to nature, the transformation rests on a paradox: that it is in the individual's best interest to put quality above his own interests. In his inquiry into the meaning of quality, Robert Pirsig offers advice that clearly has application beyond the "art of motorcycle maintenance":

> ... if [a person] takes whatever dull job he's stuck with—and they are all, sooner or later, dull—and, just to keep himself amused, starts to look for options of Quality, and secretly pursues these options, just for their own sake, thus making an art out of what he is doing, he's likely to discover that he becomes a much more interesting person and much less of an object to the people around him because his Quality decisions change *him* too. And not only the job and him, but others too because Quality tends to fan out like waves. The Quality job he didn't think anyone was going to see *is* seen, and the person who sees it feels a little better because of it, and is likely to pass that feeling on to others, and in that way the Quality tends to keep going.[8]

Appendix: The Environmental Movement

AT THE HEART of the U.S. environmental movement are about 3,000 organizations engaged in activities ranging from the preservation of scenic lands and wildlife, to pollution abatement, to the future of the human race. Several hundred of these are national or regional in scope, but the majority are local citizen groups working on issues concerning their immediate communities. Most are supported entirely by individual contributions and staffed by volunteers.

The large national organizations, however, are the most visible and familiar components of the environmental movement. These can generally be classified into two broad groups: membership organizations and professional organizations. They represent a large and varied constituency and have access to a large amount of money for use in the public interest. For example, twelve of the largest groups are supported by a total membership of over 4.3 million and have combined budgets in excess of $48 million. Their budgets are derived from a combination of individual contributions and foundation and government grants.

Professional organizations do not solicit members but usually are supported by a similar combination of private, foundation, and government donations. They engage in research, litigation, lobbying, public services, and environmental policy formation.

Groups normally classified within the population field can also be included in the environmental movement in the sense that population size and growth rates are critical to environmental quality.

The list that follows describes a sample of organizations in each of the categories discussed above—membership, professional, population—including name and address, areas of interest, size of membership (where applicable), budgets, and a contact officer. Certainly not comprehensive, the list is intended only to present a representative sample of the leading environmental organizations. Further information on the thousands of other environmental groups in the United States can be obtained from the following directories:

Gloria H. Decker (ed.), *Conservation Directory 1976, A List of Organizations, Agencies and Officials Concerned with Natural Resource Use and Management,* The National Wildlife Federation, 1412 16th Street, N.W., Washington, D.C. 20036.

Thaddeus C. Trzyna (ed.), *World Directory of Environmental Organizations, Second Edition* (1976), published for the Sierra Club by the Sequoia Institute, P.O. Box 30, Claremont, CA 91711.

Thaddeus C. Trzyna (ed.), *Environmental Protection Directory, A Comprehensive Guide to Environmental Organizations in the United States and Canada,* Second Edition (1975), published for the Center for California Public Affairs by Marquis Academic Media, 200 East Ohio Street, Chicago, Illinois 60611.

MEMBERSHIP ORGANIZATIONS

Environmental Defense Fund, 527 Madison Avenue, New York, New York 10022; (212) 593-2185. Started in 1967, EDF maintains five offices staffed by scientists, lawyers, and economists engaged in legal action, research, and public education on environmental and energy issues. Its cases have included litigation on utility rates, wildlife, toxic chemicals, water resources, highways, strip-mining, land use, pesticides, SST noise and air pollution, among others. Members: 44,000. Annual budget: $1.6 million. For further information, contact Ms. Juanita Alvarez, Information Director, 1525 18th Street, N.W., Washington, D.C. 20036.

Friends of the Earth, 529 Commercial Street, San Francisco, California 94111; (415) 391-4270. Founded in 1969, this national and international organization engages in policy research, public education, litigation, and lobbying in such areas as nuclear safety, strip-mining, Alaska land-use planning and the pipeline, ocean resources, energy conservation, and wildlife. Members: 22,000. Annual budget: $670,000. Its tax-deductible arm, Friends of the Earth Foundation,

Appendix

conducts research, public education, and public interest litigation. For further information, contact David R. Brower, President.

National Audubon Society, Inc., 950 Third Avenue, New York, New York 10022; (212) 832-3200. Founded in 1905 in the name of John James Audubon, artist, ornithologist, and conservationist, the Society is dedicated to the conservation of wildlife and the natural environment through public education and the preservation of natural areas. NAS operates six nature education centers nationwide, 68 preserves, and a Nature Center Planning Division, which provides professional advice in land and resource management. Members: 350,000. Chapters: 385. Annual budget: $8 million. For further information, contact Robert C. Boardman, Public Information Director.

National Parks and Conservation Association, 1701 18th Street, N.W., Washington, D.C. 20009; (202) 265-2717. Founded in 1919 with a view to the protection and expansion of the national park system, NPCA is a broad-program environmental organization concerned with parks, forests, wildlife, wilderness, river basins, pollution, energy, transportation, land use, and population, both at home and abroad. It works through its monthly magazine, contacts with the executive and legislative branches, litigation, and coalitions of farm, labor and conservation organizations. Members and contributors: 45,000. Annual income: $950,000. For further information, contact Crenell Mulkey, Business Manager.

National Wildlife Federation, 1412 16th Street, N.W., Washington, D.C. 20036; (202) 797-6800. The 3.5 million members of the 40-year-old Federation and its affiliated state organizations comprise the largest conservation education group in the United States. It focuses on public education, and occasional litigation and testimony, concerning wildlife and other environmental issues. Recent activities have included protection of the Big Cypress Swamp, prevention of ocean dumping, and rewards for apprehension of eagle killers. NWF's Wildlife Heritage Program offers a means for private citizens to donate land or money for natural resource preservation. Annual budget: $17 million. For further information, write to the National Wildlife Federation direct.

Natural Resources Defense Council, Inc., 15 West 44th Street, New York, New York 10036; (212) 869-0150. NRDC was established in 1970 by a group of concerned lawyers and law students with the assistance of the Ford Foundation. It is the largest environmental law firm in the

United States and undertakes research and legal action in the areas of air and water pollution, land use, mass transit, channelization, nuclear safety, national forest management, pesticides, and strip-mining. Members: 35,000. Annual budget: $1.9 million. For further information, contact Carol Hine.

The Nature Conservancy, 1800 North Kent Street, Arlington, Virginia 22209; (703) 841-5300. TNC is devoted to the preservation of ecological diversity through protection of natural areas. Since its founding in 1951, it has been instrumental in preserving over one million acres of ecologically significant land through gifts and purchase. Over 50 percent of that land has been retained in 650 sanctuaries; the balance has been turned over to local agencies or educational institutions. With TNC cooperation, ten states have set up State Natural Heritage Programs to identify and preserve their own valuable lands. Members: 28,000. Annual budget: $8.5 million for operations and acquisitions. For further information, contact Jack Lynn, Communications.

Massachusetts Audubon Society, South Great Road, Lincoln, Massachusetts, 01773; (617) 259-9500. Founded in 1896, with the primary goal of protecting birds, the society started nature education programs in 1916 and has expanded to encompass a wide range of activities in conservation, education, and research. It operates a network of wildlife sanctuaries and natural areas, an extensive environmental education program, and a small scientific staff with broad analytical capabilities. It supports local and regional conservation activities, issues several publications, and operates an environmental intern program. Members: 25,000. Annual budget: $2.4 million. For further information, contact Ms. Jane Frost, Public Information Office.

Sierra Club, 530 Bush Street, San Francisco, California 94108; (415) 981-8634. Established in 1892 by John Muir, the Sierra Club is one of the best known environmental organizations in the United States. While its major emphasis is on public education in the areas of parks and recreation, pollution control, energy, population, transportation, and land use, it also undertakes and publishes scientific studies, conducts wilderness trips, sponsors conferences and outings, engages in general conservation publishing, and maintains full-time lobbyists in Washington, D.C. and several state capitols. Related groups include the Sierra Club Legal Defense Fund, its public interest law arm; the Sierra Club Foundation, a tax-exempt organization that makes grants to the Sierra Club and other environmental groups; and a recently created political education committee. Members: 163,000. Chapters: 47. Local groups: 240. Annual budget: $7 million. For further information on the Sierra Club or any of its related activities, contact the Executive Director.

Izaak Walton League of America, 1800 North Kent Street, Arlington, Virginia 22209; (703) 528-1818. The IWL was established in 1922 to promote the protection and enjoyment of natural resources. At present, its focus is public education, policy research, citizen involvement, and legal action in the areas of water quality and the wise use of water resources and in the restoration and improvement of wildlife habitats. Members: 53,000. Annual budget: $400,000. For further information, contact the Executive Director.

The Wilderness Society, 1901 Pennsylvania Avenue, N.W., Washington, D.C. 20006; (202) 293-2732. Founded in 1935, the Society focuses on expanding and preserving the federal national wilderness system. It is concerned with sound wilderness policies, public education in wilderness values, and environmental leadership training in these areas. Much of its current work is concentrated on Alaska and the disposition of public lands under the Native Claims Settlement Act. The Society is also involved in all public land management and in the administration of the Wild and Scenic Rivers system. Members: 75,000. Annual budget: $1.7 million. For further information, contact George Davis, Executive Director.

PROFESSIONAL ORGANIZATIONS

The Conservation Foundation, 1717 Massachusetts Avenue, N.W., Washington, D.C. 20036; (202) 797-4300. CF started in 1948 and is engaged in policy research and public education in areas such as land-use planning and control, energy and growth, marine and coastal resources, water quality, and the international aspects of the environment and development. Annual budget: $1.5 million. The President is William K. Reilly.

Environmental Policy Center, 317 Pennsylvania Avenue, S.E., Washington, D.C. 20003; (202) 547-6500. EPC, founded in 1972, is a public-interest lobbying organization which specializes in legislation concerning coal- and strip-mining, off-shore oil, oil-spill liability, nuclear power, alternative energy sources, and water development projects. It is a non-membership organization which depends on public contributions for its $250,000 annual budget. Contact Louise C. Dunlap, Executive Vice President.

Scientists' Institute for Public Information, 49 East 53rd Street, New York, New York 10022; (212) 688-4050. SIPI acts as a national clearinghouse for science information on environmental integrity and public health. The SIPI publication, *Environment* magazine, has a circulation of 25,000. Members: 2,500. Annual budget: $400,000. For further information, contact Alan McGowan, President.

Worldwatch Institute, 1776 Massachusetts Avenue, N.W., Washington, D.C. 20036; (202) 452-1999. Worldwatch was created in 1974 as an independent research organization that would focus attention on a wide variety of global problems. It publishes books and a series of papers on such topics as energy, food and hunger, women, population, nuclear power, and environmental stress. Its $500,000 annual budget is obtained from private foundations, governmental agencies, and the United Nations. Dr. Lester R. Brown is President.

POPULATION ORGANIZATIONS

Planned Parenthood Federation of America, 810 Seventh Avenue, New York, New York 10019; (212) 541-7800. PPFA is the national umbrella organization of Planned Parenthood. Its 189 affiliates operate 700 clinics in 43 states and the District of Columbia. Its 1975 budget was $75 million. Jack Hood Vaughn in President.

The Population Council, 245 Park Avenue, New York, New York 10017; (212) 687-8330. The Council was founded in 1952 for scientific study and training in the population field. Its 1976 budget of $12.4 million was derived from foundation and individual contributions and from several international organizations. George Zeidenstein is President.

Zero Population Growth, 1346 Connecticut Avenue, N.W., Washington, D.C. 20036; (202) 785-0100. ZPG was established in 1968 to promote population stabilization in the United States by voluntary means. Through public education and lobbying, it advocates adoption of a comprehensive U.S. population policy and encourages reexamination of U.S. immigration policy. The ZPG Foundation is its tax-exempt arm. Members: 10,000. Chapters: 100. Annual budget: $375,000. For further information, contact Roy Morgan, Executive Director.

Notes

1. Population: How Many Is Too Many?

This chapter was drawn together by Professor Donella Meadows from contributions by Lester Brown (world population), Robert Dennis (U.S. population and immigration), and Judith Brown (immigration).

1. Lester R. Brown, "World Population Trends: Signs of Hope, Signs of Stress," Worldwatch Paper 8, Washington, D.C.: Worldwatch Institute, October 1976.
2. U.S. Department of Commerce, Bureau of the Census, *Current Population Reports,* Series P-20, No. 292, March 1976.
3. R. D. Easterlin, "On the Relation of Economic Factors to Recent and Projected Fertility Changes," *Demography,* 1966, Vol. 3, p. 131.
4. The Report of the Commission on Population Growth and the American Future, *Population and the American Future,* Washington, D.C.: U.S. Government Printing Office, 1972, p. 23.
5. R. G. Ridker, *Population, Resources, and the Environment,* U.S. Commission on Population Growth and the American Future, Vol. III, Washington, D.C.: U.S. Government Printing Office, 1972, p. 19.
6. A. Myrdal, *Nation and Family,* Cambridge, Mass.: M.I.T. Press, reprinted 1968, p. 110.
7. See *Recommendations for a New Immigration Policy for the United States,* Washington, D.C.: Zero Population Growth, 1975.

2. Food and Agriculture

This chapter was drawn together by Professor Donella Meadows primarily from materials provided by Lester Brown and David Pimentel, and from her own work.

1. Lester R. Brown, "The Politics and Responsibility of the North American Breadbasket," Worldwatch Paper 2, Washington, D.C.: Worldwatch Institute, October 1975.
2. Brown, "World Population Trends."
3. E. P. Eckholm, *Losing Ground, Environmental Stress and World Food Prospects,* New York: W. W. Norton & Co., 1976.
4. Stephen Schneider, deputy head of the climate project at the National Center for Atmospheric Research, discusses this problem of national policies to stabilize food availability in his recent book *The Genesis Strategy,* New York: Plenum, 1976.
5. M. Mesarovic and E. Pestel, *Mankind at the Turning Point: The Second Report to the Club of Rome,* New York: E. P. Dutton/Reader's Digest Press, 1974, p. 122. Also see "World Food and Nutrition Study," Interim Report, National Academy of Sciences, Washington, D.C., 1975.
6. Brown, "Politics and Responsibility of the North American Breadbasket," p. 11.
7. This is drawn from an extended discussion of possible approaches presented by Donella Meadows in "Food and Population: Policies for the United States," in David Baldwin, *America in a Changing World,* Hanover, N.H.: University Press of New England, 1976.
8. Brown, "Politics and Responsibility of the North American Breadbasket," p. 36. It should be noted that the U.S. and Canada together are the only major sources of exportable food. Differences between these two countries may develop on food policy. Unless a new energy strategy is followed, the U.S. will face enormous balance of payment problems as a result of its oil-import bill. Since food sales provide such a large fraction of U.S. foreign exchange, balancing our foreign accounts would require America to grow as much food as possible and to sell to the highest bidder. Canada is self-sufficient in energy and therefore not faced with the same problem. Nonetheless, the two nations should be able to agree on a common policy for access to the North American food market.
9. Richard Barnet and R. Muller, *Global Reach: The Power of Multinational Corporations,* New York: Simon & Schuster, 1974.
10. H. Linnemann, "Fourth Report to the Club of Rome," Amsterdam, The Netherlands: in press.
11. Production Yearbook, United Nations Food and Agriculture Organization, Vol. 28-1 (1974).

Notes

12. An excellent discussion of this problem is provided in the October 8, 1976, issue of *Science,* "Land Degradation: Effects on Food and Energy Resources," by David Pimentel *et al.,* pp. 149-155. Another discussion can be found in the short report by Roger Blobaum, "The Loss of Agricultural Land," Washington, D.C.: Citizens' Advisory Committee on Environmental Quality, 1974.
13. For examples, see such publications as *Appropriate Technology* (a quarterly from Intermediate Technology Publications, Ltd., 9 King Street, London WC2E8HN) and *Coevolution Quarterly,* Box 428, Sausalito, Calif. 94965.
14. For examples from developing countries, see Keith Griffin, *The Political Economy of Agrarian Change,* Cambridge, Mass.: Harvard University Press, 1974, pp. 38, 42, 59. For data from the U.S., Japan, and India, see Kusum Nair, *The Lonely Furrow,* Ann Arbor: University of Michigan Press, 1969; Warren R. Bailey, "The One-Man Farm," Economic Research Service, U.S. Department of Agriculture, 1973; and the *Journal of the New Alchemists,* Vols. 1,2,3, Woods Hole, Mass.: The New Alchemy Institute.
15. A good summary of the impending problems of energy-intensive agriculture and food systems is provided by Gerald Leach in *Energy and Food Production,* 1975, International Institute for Environment and Development, 1525 New Hampshire Avenue, N.W., Washington, D.C. 20036. Also see *Food Policy,* Volume 1, No. 1, published quarterly by IPC Science and Technology Press, Ltd., 32 High Street, Guildford, Surrey, England GU1 3EW. The problem in developing countries is discussed in "Energy Use in Rural India," by Roger Revell, *Science,* June 4, 1976, p. 969.
16. See, for example, William Lockeretz *et al.,* "A Comparison of the Production, Economic Returns, and Energy Intensiveness of Corn Belt Farms That Do and Do Not Use Inorganic Fertilizers and Pesticides," Washington University, St. Louis: Center for the Biology of Natural Systems, July 1975.

3. The Energy Economy

This chapter was written by Amory B. Lovins and draws heavily on his paper "Energy Strategy: The Road Not Taken?" in *Foreign Affairs,* October1976, pp. 65-96. That paper contains a fuller and more heavily annotated exposition than is possible here.

1. See Lovins, "Energy Strategy."
2. According to a recent Stanford Research Institute study (see note

20 below), "In 1974, federal subsidies for energy included $1.2 billion for the investment tax credit for utilities, $3 billion for other energy tax subsidies, $2 billion for interest on past government energy investments, and $0.2 billion for ERDA energy R&D—an energy subsidy of more than $5 billion. In 1976, the total energy subsidy approaches $8 billion, not including indirect energy subsidies such as those for highways, airports, and property tax exemption of publicly owned energy utilities such as the Tennessee Valley Authority and the Booneville Power Administration." In "Investment Planning in the Energy Sector," LBL-4479, Berkeley, Calif.: March 1, 1976, Lawrence Berkeley Laboratory, E. Kahn *et al.,* estimate that the taxpayer subsidy on new power stations is now 20 percent—half by investment tax credit and half by accelerated depreciation allowance.

3. The foregoing data are based on ERDA-48 and ERDA-76-1 (the 1975 and 1976 ERDA RD&D plans respectively), and on M. Carasso *et al., The Energy Supply Planning Model,* PB-245 382 and PB-245 383, Springfield, Va.: National Technical Information Service, a Bechtel Corp. report to the National Science Foundation, August 1975.

4. M. Flood, "Nuclear Sabotage," *Bulletin of the Atomic Scientists,* in press.

5. Informative and carefully documented reports on the Browns Ferry fire and on many other aspects of U.S. reactor safety are published by the Union of Concerned Scientists, 1208 Massachusetts Avenue, Cambridge, Mass. 02138.

6. See A. B. Lovins and J. H. Price, *Non-Nuclear Futures: The Case for an Ethical Energy Strategy,* Cambridge, Mass.: Ballinger/Friends of the Earth, 1975, especially Appendix I-2.

7. See R. Gillette, *Science,* 181:728 (1973).

8. M. Willrich and T. Taylor, *Nuclear Theft: Risks and Safeguards,* Cambridge, Mass.: Ballinger, 1974; D. M. Rosenbaum, *et al.,* "A Special Safeguards Study," Internal Task Force Report to the director of licensing, USAEC, 1974; reprinted in 120 Congr. Rec. S6621-30 (April 30, 1974); John McPhee, *The Curve of Binding Energy,* New York: Farrar, Straus, & Giroux, 1974. See also D. Burnham, *New York Times,* December 29, 1974, p. 26, in which it is stated that "there already were two known instances where Government employees were discovered to have smuggled out of guarded facilities enough special nuclear materials to fashion a nuclear weapon." A carefully worded denial appears in

USAEC Press Release U-3, Jan. 2, 1975. A well-documented 1970 case of nuclear blackmail by a 14-year-old schoolboy without any strategic material is described by R. Lapp, *New York Times Magazine,* February 4, 1973; and by T. H. Ingram, *Washington Monthly,* December 1972, p. 20.

9. General Accounting Office report, "Assessment of U.S. and International Controls over Peaceful Uses of Nuclear Energy," publication number ID-76-60, September 14, 1976.
10. Senate Government Operations Committee report, "Facts on Nuclear Proliferation," December 1975, Congressional Research Service, Library of Congress; Albert Wohlstetter *et al.,* "Moving Toward Life in a Nuclear Armed Crowd," report ACDA/PAB-263 to Arms Control and Disarmament Agency, U.S. State Department, April 22, 1976, prepared by Pan Heuristics, 1801 Avenue of the Stars, Suite 1221, Los Angeles, Calif. 90067; a 1975 report to ERDA (ERDA-52) systematically demolishes the bizarre notion that nuclear power is technically or economically appropriate for developing countries.
11. R. Ayres, *10 Harv. Civ. Rights—Civ. Lib. L. Rev.,* 369-443 (Spring 1975); J. H. Barton, "Intensified Nuclear Safeguards and Civil Liberties," report to USNRC, Stanford Law School, October 21, 1975.
12. Lovins and Price, *Non-Nuclear Futures,* and references cited therein.
13. H. P. Green, *43 Geo. Wash. L. Rev.,* 791-807 (March 1975).
14. I. C. Bupp and J. C. Derain, "Nuclear Reactor Safety: the Twilight of Probability," December 1975; available from Professor Bupp, Harvard Business School.
15. Lovins sketches this case in his Introduction to "Facts on Nuclear Proliferation" (see note 10 above), supported by the independent Danish work of B. Sørenson, *Science,* 189:225-60 (1975), and by his own calculation, checked by Canadian authorities, for Canada (*Conserver Society Notes,* June 1976, pp. 3-16, Science Council of Canada, 150 Kent, Ottawa). Extensive supporting data appear in the interim (Autumn 1976) and final (1976-77) reports of the U.S. energy study of the Union of Concerned Scientists (see note 5). Similar projects are underway in the EEC, Sweden, Denmark, the United Kingdom, Austria, Israel, and elsewhere; all so far are yielding results consistent with these conclusions.
16. The hazards of too much energy include not only climatic limits to heat release (generally expected to become acute within the next

half to two-thirds of a century at historical growth rates) and the ecological effects of energy use (P. Ehrlich, "An Ecologist's Perspective on Nuclear Power," Federation of American Scientists Public Interest Report, Vol. 28, no. 5-6, May-June, 1975), but also the previously sketched structural effects of high-energy, high-technology systems on the social and political fabric. As Lovins points out in "Energy Strategy," the potential for largely escaping limitations of fuel resources is one reason not to favor development of controlled nuclear fusion. Other reasons—technical, economic, and geopolitical—are outlined both by Lovins and, more technically, by W. D. Metz, *Science,* 192:1320-3, 193:38-40, 76, 193:307-9 (1976). Most environmentalists who have considered these arguments would now agree that fusion research, ERDA's second largest money consumer, should not continue to be highly funded. Enthusiasm for fusion among environmentalists is now largely confined to those who erroneously believe that fusion will be cheap, environmentally benign, and free of safeguards and social problems.

17. Lovins states representative costs (see "Energy Strategy"), worked out in detail in his "Scale, Centralization, and Electrification in Energy Systems," *Future Strategies of Energy Development,* symposium, Oak Ridge Associated Universities, Oak Ridge, Tn., October 20-21, 1976. Of course, even if soft systems were not cheaper, they would have enormous non-economic advantages most of which cannot be quantified.
18. Lovins, "Energy Strategy."
19. Lovins, in "Facts on Nuclear Proliferation" (see note 10 above).
20. "A Preliminary Social and Environmental Assessment of the ERDA Solar Energy Program 1975-2020," Stanford Research Institute study for ERDA, Solar Energy Division, Menlo Park, Calif: in press.
21. Ibid.
22. The Princeton University group studying plutonium economy for the Ford Foundation makes a strong case for suspending implementation of a plutonium economy. See the series of papers by Drs. William Von Hippel, Taylor, and Feiveson, *Bulletin of the Atomic Scientists,* in press.
23. Most parts of the U.S. have substantial overcapacity, plus large increments of nuclear and fossil capacity, under construction which will come on-line between now and about 1985. By then, conserva-

tion can start to bite and it will be possible to have over 50 GW (e) of cogeneration capacity operating (Dow Chemical Co. *et al.,* "Industrial Energy Center Study," PB-243 824, NTIS, report to NSF, June 1975). Phasing out nuclear power—which has just passed firewood as a national energy source—should be relatively painless if combined with conservation and cogeneration. For illustration (California), see R. Doctor *et al., Sierra Club Bulletin,* May 1976, pp. 4ff.

4. Natural Resources: Will They Last?

This chapter was written by Ian Nisbet based on an early draft by Charles Ryan. Although it deals primarily with materials problems of the United States, there are corresponding problems in the developing world. Nathan Keyfitz's article "World Resources and the World Middle Class," *Scientific American,* July 1976, is an excellent introduction to the world resource problem. An analysis is badly needed of the world resource situation as it relates to the resource needs of developing nations if they are to succeed in their economic plans in the decades ahead.

1. T. S. Lovering, "Mineral Resources from the Land," in *Resources and Man: A Study and Recommendations* by the Committee on Resources and Man of the Division of Earth Sciences, National Academy of Sciences—National Research Council, with the cooperation of the Division of Biology and Agriculture, San Francisco: W. H. Freeman, 1969, p. 116.

5. Water and Air Pollution

This chapter was written by Gerald Barney from drafts provided by J. Clarence Davies III, Judith L. Brown, and others.

1. The Council on Environmental Quality, *Environmental Quality—1975,* Executive Office of the President, Washington, D.C.: Government Printing Office, December 1975, p. 326.
2. Ibid., pp. 352, 355.
3. Report to the Congress by the National Commission on Water Quality, Washington, D.C.: Government Printing Office, March 18, 1976.
4. Comptroller General of the United States, *Implementing the National Water Pollution Control Permit Program: Progress and Problem,* Washington, D.C.: General Accounting Office No. RED-76-60, February 9, 1976.

THE UNFINISHED AGENDA

6. The Hazards of Toxic Substances

This chapter was written by Joseph Highland and Arlie Schardt.

1. Sixth Annual Report of the Council on Environmental Quality, December 1975; World Health Organization, *Prevention of Cancer,* Technical Report, Series 276, Geneva: W.H.O., 1974.
2. *National Cancer Institute Fact Book,* HEW Publication No. (NIH) 76-512, December, 1975.
3. Sixth Annual Report of the Council on Environmental Quality, December 1975.
4. Joseph F. Fraumeni, Jr. (ed.), *Persons at High Risk of Cancer: An Approach to Cancer Etiology and Control,* New York: Academic Press, 1975.
5. Among the principal federal laws to control environmental pollution are: Clean Air Act; Federal Water Pollution Control Act; Safe Drinking Water Act; Occupational Safety and Health Act; Consumer Product Safety Act; Food, Drug and Cosmetic Act; Federal Insecticide, Fungicide and Rodenticide Act; Energy Research and Development Act.
6. Authority to implement the foregoing and other related laws is shared, *inter alia,* by the Environmental Protection Agency, the Food and Drug Administration, the Occupational Safety and Health Administration, the Nuclear Regulatory Commission, and the Consumer Product Safety Commission.
7. *National Conference on Polychlorinated Biphenyls* (November 19-21, 1975, Chicago), Conference Proceedings, Environmental Protection Agency, Office of Toxic Substances, Washington, D.C.: 1976; *Criteria Document for Toxic Pollutant Effluent Standards for PCBs,* Environmental Protection Agency, Washington, D.C.: August 1976.
8. M. Kuratsune, "Epidemiologic Study on Yusho, a Poisoning Caused by Rice Oil Contaminated with a Commercial Brand of Polychlorinated Biphenyls," *Envir. Health Perspect.,* 1:119, 1972; M. Kuratsune, "An Abstract of Results of Laboratory Examinations of Patients with Yusho and of Animal Experiments," *Envir. Health Perspect.,* 1:129, 1972.
9. R. D. Kimbrough *et al.,* "Induction of Liver Tumors in Sherman Strain Female Rats by Polychlorinated Biphenyl Aroclor 1260," Center for Disease Control, Atlanta, Ga., in press; *General Criteria for Assessing the Evidence for Carcinogenicity of Chemical Substances,* National Cancer Institute, June 1976.

10. *Forward Plan for Health,* fiscal years 1977-1981, Department of Health, Education and Welfare, Public Health Service, Washington, D.C.: June 1975.

7. Spaceship Earth: The Life-Support System

This chapter was written by Donella Meadows from an initial draft prepared by Katharine Smith. Other contributors include Ian Nisbet, Laurance Rockefeller, George Davis, Thomas Kimball, Maitland Sharpe, Anthony Wayne Smith, Elvis Stahr and William Reilly.

1. Aldo Leopold, *A Sand County Almanac,* New York: Oxford University Press, 1966, pp. 237-264.

8. The New Biological Threat

This chapter was written by Nicholas Wade.

1. *Draft Environmental Impact Statement for Guidelines for Research Involving Recombinant DNA Molecules,* Bethesda, Maryland: NIH, August 1976, P. Berg, *et al.,* "Potential Biohazards of Recombinant DNA Molecules," *Science,* 185:303, 1974; P. Berg *et al.,* "Summary Statement of the Asilomar Conference on Recombinant DNA Molecules," *Science,* 189:991, 1975.
2. "Recombinant DNA Research," *Federal Register,* July 7, 1976, pp. 27902-27943.
3. D. A. Jackson *et al.,* "Biochemical Method for Inserting New Genetic Information into DNA of Simian Virus 40: Circular SV 40 Molecules Containing Lambda Phage Genes and the Galactose Operon of Escherichia Coli," *Proc. Nat. Acad. Sci.,* 69, 10, 2904-9, October 1972.
4. R. Sinsheimer, "Troubled Dawn for Genetic Engineering," *New Scientist,* October 16, 1975; "Recombinant DNA: The Last Look Before the Leap," *Science,* 192:236-8, 1976.
5. A. G. Wedum, "The Detrick Experience as a Guide to the Probable Efficacy of P4 Microbiological Containment for Studies on Microbial Recombinant DNA Facilities," unpublished report to the National Cancer Institute, 1976.
6. A. M. Chakrabarty, "Which Way Genetic Engineering?" *Industrial Research,* January 1976, pp. 45-50.
7. Miranda Robertson, "ICI Puts Money on Genetic Engineering," *Nature,* 251: 564-565, October 18, 1974.
8. Quoted in *Science,* 193: 215, 1976.

9. "Polyoma and SV40 Virus," *Proposed Guidelines for Research Involving Recombinant DNA Molecules,* Appendix B., Bethesda, Maryland: National Institute of Health, January 1976; Janice Crossland, "Hands on the Code," *Environment,* Vol. 18, Number 7, September 1976, pp. 6-16.

9. Society and Decision-Making

This chapter was written primarily by Gerald Barney, with contributions from Ian Nisbet, Amory B. Lovins, Donella Meadows, J. Clarence Davies III, and other members of the Task Force and project advisors.

1. Several of the suggestions in this section are drawn from a 1976 speech on national planning given by J. Irwin Miller to the Conference Board.
2. In the environmental area alone, a brief paragraph on each of the government's many environmental data-collection efforts results in a book of more than 100 pages—*The Federal Environmental Monitoring Directory,* prepared by the Council on Environmental Quality, Washington, D.C.: Government Printing Office, May 1973.
3. This series of reports has improved markedly in quality and shows promise of further improvement now that the process of preparation is open to public input. (The early reports were prepared as if they were clandestine C.I.A. operations.) The latest report in the series is "1976 Report on National Growth and Development: The Changing Issues for National Development," prepared under the direction of the Committee on Community Development of the Domestic Council, February 1976.
4. E. F. Schumacher, *Small Is Beautiful,* New York: Harper and Row, 1973, p. 39.
5. Leopold, *A Sand County Almanac,* p. 93.
6. Nan Robertson, "French Drive On to Reduce Waste," *The New York Times,* p. 10, July 23, 1976.
7. A certain amount of progress is now being made toward this synthesis. For example, see: Nicholas Georgescu-Roegen, *The Entropy Law and the Economic Process,* Cambridge, Mass.: Harvard University Press, 1971; *AIP Conference Proceedings No. 25, Efficient Use of Energy,* American Institute of Physics, 1975; Special Issue on Energy Analysis, *Energy Policy,* Vol. 3, Number

4, IPC Science and Technology Press Ltd., December 1975; *Workshop Report,* International Federation of Institutes for Advanced Study, Workshop on Energy Analysis and Economics, Lidingo, Sweden, June 22-27, 1975.
8. A broad discussion of the curricular changes needed in higher education is now available in: *Growth and Education: A Strategic Report to the Rockefeller Brothers Fund on the Implications of Growth Policy for Postsecondary Education,* Boulder, Colorado: Western Interstate Commission for Higher Education, December 1974; and in Lewis J. Perelman, *The Global Mind, Beyond the Limits to Growth,* New York: Mason/Charter, 1976.
9. Information from the National Broadcasting Corporation, New York, based on NBC 1975 data.
10. Data provided by the Television Information Office, New York.
11. Robert M. Liebert *et al., The Early Window: The Effects of Television on Children and Youth,* New York: Pergamon Press, 1973.

10. A Question of Values

This chapter was written by Gerald Barney on the basis of a first draft by Amory Lovins and with numerous comments and suggestions from members of the Task Force, advisors, and editors.
1. Garrett Hardin, "The Tragedy of the Commons," *Science,* December 13, 1968, 162, pp. 1234-1248.
2. See the following: Jay W. Forrester, *World Dynamics,* Cambridge, Mass.: Wright-Allen Press, Inc., 1971; D. H. Meadows *et al., The Limits to Growth,* New York: Universe Books, 1972; D. H. Meadows *et al., The Dynamics of Growth in a Finite World,* Cambridge, Mass.: Wright-Allen Press, 1974; A. B. Lovins, "Long-Term Constraints on Human Activity," *Environmental Conservation, 3,* 1, 3-14, Geneva: 1976.
3. For a more detailed discussion of the value transformation to an environmental or land ethic, see: W. W. Harman, "Notes on the Coming Transformation," Stanford Research Institute, unpublished paper, February 1975; O. W. Markley *et al., Changing Images of Man,* Stanford Research Institute, Research Project Report 2150, October 1973; Robert Cahn, "The Environmental Ethic," in *Critical Choices for Americans VI: Values of Growth,* New York: D. C. Heath and Co., 1976.

4. Herman Daly, *Toward a Steady State Society,* San Francisco: Freeman Press, 1974.
5. For example, see Lynn White, Jr., "The Historic Roots of Our Ecologic Crisis," *Science,* March 10, 1969, *155,* pp. 1203-1207.
6. Just why such questions evoke heated reactions has been explored in a fascinating essay in U. S. Reuyl *et al.,* "Key Insights and Issues," in *A Preliminary Social and Environmental Assessment of the ERDA Solar Energy Program 1975-2020,* Vol. 1., Stanford, Calif.: Stanford Research Institute, 1976. A less controversial analysis is Thomas S. Kuhn, *The Structure of Scientific Revolutions,* 2nd ed., Chicago: University of Chicago Press, 1970.
7. Aldo Leopold, *Sand County Almanac* p. 264.
8. Robert Pirsig, *Zen and the Art of Motorcycle Maintenance,* New York: William Morrow and Co., 1974, p. 357.

Index

Abortion, 12, 29, 38
Acid sulfates, 89-90
Actinides, 54
Aesthetics, and environment, 159-60
Agriculture. *See* Food and agriculture
Agricultural lands, nonconversion of, 14, 43-4, 118
Agricultural technology, intermediate, 14-15, 44-7, 65
Agriculture Department, 106
Air pollution, 17, 89, 93; evaluation and regulation of, 81-90; recommendations for, 17, 88-90
Alaska, 100, 109; wilderness of, 19, 110-13
Alaska Native Claims Settlement Act (1971), 102, 111-12
Alaska Statehood Act (1958), 112
Aliens, immigration of, 13, 24, 32-3
Antimony, 75
Antitrust laws, 21, 147; and energy policy, 16, 67
Army Corps of Engineers, 78, 79, 107
Arsenic, 88, 93
Asbestos, 88
Asilomar Conference, 128, 129
Automobiles, 17, 72-4, 89

Balanced Growth and Economic Planning Act, 136-7
Beef production, 46
Beryllium, 75, 76
Beverage containers, 17, 72

Bimetallics, 71, 72
Biological weapons, 126, 130
Biomedical research, 97-8. *See also* Recombinant DNA technique
Biotic diversity, 19, 101-2, 107-10
Birth defects and mutations, 93-4, 98
Birth rates, 14, 38
Bureau of Land Management, 103, 105-6, 108
Bureau of Reclamation, 78-9, 107

Cadmium, 73, 91, 97
Cancer research, 18, 92-3, 96-8
Carcinogens, 53, 86, 92-5
Cars, 74, 89; recycling of, 17, 72-3
Cesium, 97
Chemical screening, 18, 93, 96-8
Chlorination substitutes, 86
Chromium, 73, 75
Cigarette smoking, 18, 93, 98
City planning, 137-9. *See also* National planning
Clean Air Act Amendments (1970), 17, 81, 84, 87
Climate changes, 36, 53, 118-19
Coal, 51, 53, 148; conversion methods, 15, 62-63, 65, 77, 155
Cobalt, 75
Coliform bacteria, 82
Commerce Department, and SSE, 21, 150
Commercials, 22, 152-4
Composting, 48

Index

Congress: and immigration, 13, 33; and land use, 116–17; and pollution, 17, 84–7; and wilderness preservation, 19, 105–6, 112
Conservation: of energy, 59–62, 65; of resources, 16–17, 60–1, 71, 75–6, 80
Conservation Directory, The, 162
Conservation Foundation, The, 165
"Conserver Society," as U.S. goal, 16, 71, 157
Contraception, 12, 28–9, 37–8
Copper, 71, 73, 75, 91
Corn production, 45
Council on Environmental Quality (CEQ), 22, 81–3, 142, 146–7

d-2 lands, 112
Daycare centers, 12, 30
Death rates, 14, 38
Decision-making, 20–2, 132–54; and Federal agency organization, 142–4; and national planning, 133–9; and private sector, 132, 144–50; and technology assessment, 139–42
Defense Department, 128
Department of Natural Resources (proposed), 143–4
Deposits, refundable, 17, 72; on cars, 72–3
DES, 93
Disposal, 17, 21, 72–3
DNA. *See* Recombinant DNA technique
Durability standards, 16–17, 71, 74, 147

E. coli, 86; and DNA research, 20, 124–5, 128–30
Economic indicator revision, 21, 149
Economics: of energy, 50–68; and environment, 21–2, 145–50; of nuclear energy, 16, 65, 67; and private sector decision-making, 144–50; of recycling, 71–4; of resource depletion, 69–72, 150. *See also* SSE

Ecosystem preservation, 18–19, 99–122; and "land ethic," 120–2; and private lands, 115–18; and public lands, 100–15; U.S. role in, 118–20
Education: demographic, 12, 31; environmental, 21–2, 151–4
Effluent fees, 84
Electricity reduction, 15, 51–3, 59–61, 65
Emission control systems, 75–6
Endangered species, protection of, 107–10
Endangered Species Act (1973), 19, 108–9
Energy, 14, 51, 74; conservation of, 59–62, 65; economics of, 50–68; end-use, 15, 51, 58–61; and food production, 44–7; income sources, 15, 59–60, 62, 148; production changes, 15, 51–3, 61–2; Project Independence and, 51–3, 58; and resource depletion, 69–71; soft-technologies, 59–60, 62–4; U.S. policy (proposed), 15–16, 59–68; waste of, 52, 59, 150. *See also* Nuclear energy
Environment: and aesthetics, 159–60; cancer and, 92–3; and chemical fertilizer, 47–8; economics of, 21–2, 145–50; education on, 21–2, 151–4; and federal agencies, 142–4; and national planning, 136–7; as national priority, 21, 142–4; and natural resources, 69; and nuclear energy, 55; of soft energy, 63–4; and technology assessment, 142
Environmental Defense Fund, 162
Environmental organizations, 161–6
Environmental Policy Center, 165
Environmental Protection Agency. *See* EPA
Environmental Protection Directory, 162
EPA (Environmental Protection Agency), 17, 81, 89, 153; and air quality, 87–9; and toxic sub-

stances, 96-7; and water quality, 83, 85-7
Equity, 157
Escherichia coli. *See E. coli*
Eutrophication, 48, 83
External combustion engine, 89

Family education programs, 12, 29, 30
Family planning, 12, 27, 29, 30-2, 37
Federal agencies, reorganization of, 142-4
Feedback, 135, 150
Fertility rates, 12, 25, 26, 38
Fertilizer, 41; chemical, 14, 47-9, 155; organic, 14, 47, 48-9; sludge as, 90-1
Flora and fauna. *See* Wildlife preservation
Fluid fuels, 50, 52, 65
Fluorocarbons, 119, 133-4, 155
Food and agriculture, 13-14, 34-49; and additives, 92, 93; PCBs in, 94-6
Food and Drug Administration, 139
Food consumption, U.S., 27, 40-1, 45-6
Food production, 34, 36-7; energy for, 44; increase in, 13, 14, 37, 42-7
Food redistribution, 13, 36-7, 39-42
Forecasting, 135
Foreign aid, 41-2; and immigration, 13, 33; and population, 12, 27, 38
Forest preservation, 118, 120, 147
Forest Service, 102, 105-6, 108, 114-15
Forward Plan for Health (HEW), 96-7
Fossil fuels, 53, 75, 97, 148; as bridge, 15, 59, 62; conservation of, 60-1; for plastics, 76-7
Friends of the Earth, 162
Fuel alcohol industry, 15, 62, 65
Fuel-economy standards, 16, 41, 66
Fusion technology, 56-7, 65

Garbage, as fertilizer, 47, 48
Gasoline tax, 15, 66

General Electric, and DNA research, 127
Genetic diversity, 19, 101-2, 107-10
GNP (Gross National Product), 69, 148-9
Government: and decision-making, 132, 133-44; and energy economy, 51-3, 66; and family planning, 25, 28-30; and federal agency organization, 142-4; and nuclear energy, 55-8; and pollution, 83, 94; and private land-use, 115-18
Groundwater recharging, 79
Growth, rethinking of, 157

Habitat preservation, 18-19, 107-10
Hardin, Garrett, 156
Hawaii, 100, 120
Health hazards, toxic substances as, 93-6
Heavy metals, 53, 91
Helium, 70, 76
HUD (Housing and Urban Development), 89, 135, 138-9

Immigration, 13, 24, 32-3
Imperial Chemicals Industries, Ltd., 127-8
Incentives, for nonpollution, 83-4
Insurance, 139
Interdependence, and value changes, 155-60
Interior Department, 106, 108, 112
Interstate highway system, 16, 66
Island ecosystem preservation, 19, 120
Izaac Walton League of America, 165

Jackson, Henry, 116-17

Kepone, 93, 98

Labor, and agriculture, 45-6, 49
Laboratories, monitoring of, 20, 98, 127-8, 129
Land: private, 115-18; public acquisition of, 102-13; public management of, 100-2, 113-15

Land and Water Conservation Fund, 104
"Land ethic," development of, 19, 121-2
Land preservation: for agriculture, 14, 43-4, 118; importance of, 101-2
Land-use planning, 43-4, 53, 89; for private land, 115-18; for public land, 102-15
Law of the Sea Conference (U.N.), 110
Lead, 91, 97; airborne, 87, 88
Leopold, Aldo, 121, 145, 160
Life-support system, Earth as, 18-19, 99-122
Lithium, 57
Lovering, Thomas, 75

Manganese, 75
Marine mammals, 19, 110
Marine species, protection of, 110
Massachusetts Audubon Society, 164
Mass transit, 15, 65, 89
Material. *See* Mineral extraction; Natural resources
Mercury, 70, 75, 76, 85, 97
Mineral extraction: and ecology, 105-6, 108, 114-15; and energy, 70-1; geopolitics and, 74-6. *See also* Natural resources
Mining: seabed, 110; and wilderness preservation, 105-6
Mining Law of 1872, 19, 114-15

National Audubon Society, Inc., 163
National Cancer Institute, 98
National Commission of Water Quality, 78, 85
National Environmental Policy Act, 142-3
National Forest Management Act (1976), 115
National Forests, 100, 112, 114-15
National Growth Reports, 135
National Institutes of Health (NIH), 124, 126-9, 131
National Parks and Conservation Association, 163

National Parks system, 100, 102-3, 112, 113-14, 120
National planning, 20; accountability/independence question, 135-7; analysis techniques for, 135, 150; and Balanced Growth and Economic Planning Act, 136-7; for cities, 137-9; and decision-making, 133-9; Presidential commission on (proposed), 136-7; and private land regulation, 115-18; and SSE, 149-50
National Planning Board (proposed), 136-7
National Science Foundation (NSF): and city planning, 138-9; and SSE, 21, 150; and TV, 22, 153
National Wildlife Federation, 163
National Wildlife Refuge system, 102, 107-10, 112
National Wildlife Refuge System Administrative Act (1966), 107-8
Natural gas, 41, 50, 51, 76; tax on, 147-8
Natural resources, 16-17, 69-80, 111; conservation of, 60-1, 71; economics of, 69-72; foreign sources of, 75-76; and population, 26-7; recycling of, 71-4; reuse of, 74; water as, 77-80. *See also* Mineral extraction
Natural Resources Defense Council, Inc., 163
Nature Conservancy, The, 164
Nerve gas, 140
Nickel, 75, 91
Niobium, 75, 76
Nitrates, 88, 89
Nonpoint pollution, 83, 85-6, 90
Nuclear energy, 53-8, 140-1; economics of, 16, 65, 67; fusion technology and, 56-7, 65; nonexportation of, 66-7; phasing out of, 15, 16, 66-7; political impact of, 55-8; and radioactive waste, 54, 56-7; safety of, 53-6; subsidies for, 16, 67; and terrorism, 54-6, 140. *See also* Energy

Index

Ocean ecosystems, 110
Office of Technology Assessment, 52, 139
Office of the Comptroller General, 137
Oil, 50-1, 53, 147
Oil shale, 52, 53, 65
Omnibus Rivers and Harbors Bill, 79
Ores, availability of, 75-6
Organic Act of 1976, 106
Organic waste, 44, 48, 62, 65
Ozone layer, 48, 89, 119, 134

Palladium, 75
Particulates, 82; fine, 88, 89
PCBs, 18, 85, 94-6
Pest control, biological, 14, 44, 49
Pesticides, 49, 92, 93, 95
Phosphates, 133
Pirsig, Robert, 160
Planned obsolescence, 73, 147
Planned Parenthood Federation of America, 166
Plastics, use and recycling of, 77
Platinum, 75
Plutonium, 55, 56, 67
"Plutonium Connection, The" (TV program), 140
Point source pollution, 82, 85-6, 90
Pollution. *See* Air pollution; Water pollution
Population, 11-13, 23-33, 38; and city planning, 138-9; and food shortages, 35-6; global stabilization of, 13, 37-9; and immigration, 32-3; recommendations for U.S. policy, 12-13, 26-7, 28-33, 38-9; and resource access, 26-7
Population Council, The, 166
Population organizations, 166
Price-Anderson Act, 66
Private sector decision-making, 132, 144-50
Product durability. *See* Durability standards
Project Independence, 51-3, 58
Property-tax reform, 44
Public, U.S. *See* Society

Quality, 26, 160

Radioactive waste, 54, 56-7
Railroads, 15, 16, 65
Rare-earth elements, 17, 76
Recombinant DNA technique, 19-20, 123-31, 140; code of ethics for, 130-1; guidelines for, 20, 124, 126-9, 131; hazards of, 124-6; restriction of, 20, 127-30
Recycling, 71-4; and pollution, 71, 73, 74; of resources, 15, 16-17, 75-7; of sewage, 86; of water, 79
Red Dye No. 2, 93
Regression analysis, 135
Repair, of products, 21, 73, 147
Resource economics, 150
Resources. *See* Natural resources
Reuse of resources, 16, 71, 74, 79. *See also* Recycling
River preservation, 106-7

Schumacher, E. F., 145
Scientists' Institute for Public Information, 166
Seabed mining, 110
Securities laws, and energy industry, 16, 67
Sewage treatment, 48, 79, 86-7, 90-1, 133
Sex education, 12, 29
Shoreland preservation, 107
Sierra Club, 164
Silver, 75, 76
Sinsheimer theory, 126
Sludge, 90-1, 133; as fertilizer, 47-8, 90-1
Smoking, 18, 93, 98
Society: and decision-making, 20-2, 132-54; and energy policy, 15, 66; and value changes, 155-60
Soil conservation, 14, 43
Solar grain driers, 44, 47
Solar space-conditioning, 15, 62, 65
Solar technology, 57, 59, 63
Spaceship Earth. *See* Ecosystem preservation
Speed limit, national, 16, 66

SSE (steady state economy), 21, 149–50
SST (airplane), 119, 140
State parks, 102, 104
Steady state economy (SSE), 21, 149–50
Sterilization, 12, 29, 38
Strip-mining, 51, 65, 148
Subsidies: to energy industries, 16, 67, 146–7; to recycling industries, 73–4
Sulfates, 88, 89
Sulfur dioxide, 82, 84, 88, 89–90
Supreme Court, 137
SV 40 (cancer virus), 130
Synthetics, recycling of, 77
Systems analysis, 135, 150

Taxes: on cigarettes, 40, 98; on emissions, 84; and environment, 146; and family planning, 12, 30, 32; on food, 40; on gasoline, 15, 66; on property, 44; and recycling industry, 73–4; on resources, 147–8; on seabed mining, 110
Technology control, 21, 139–42
Television, 21-2, 151-4
Timber industry, 100, 105–6, 108, 114–15
Toxic substances, 18, 92–8, 124, 139; and product disposal, 72–3; in sewage, 86–7, 91; in water, 82–3, 86–7
Toxic Substances Control Act (1976), 18, 96–7
Trace metals, in water, 83
Trade, international, 42
"Tragedy of the Commons, The" (Hardin), 156
Transportation Department, 89
Tritium, radioactive, 57
Tropical rain forest preservation, 118–20
Tungsten, 75, 76

Udall, Morris, 116–17
Uranium, 52, 75, 97

Urban parks, 104
Urban restoration, 117
U.S.-Canada Commission on Food Policy (proposed), 14, 39–40
Utility price structure, 16, 67

Value changes, 155–60
Vanadium, 75
Vinyl chloride, 93

Waste heat, 53, 61, 78
Waste management, 15, 47, 65; organic, 44, 48, 62, 82–3; radioactive, 54, 56–7
Water: engineering projects, 78, 79, 106–7; Indian rights to, 78, 80; as natural resource, 77–80; shortages of, 53, 78
Water pollution, 17, 48, 77, 93; evaluation and regulation of, 81–90; recommendations for, 17, 84–7; and waste heat, 78
Water Pollution Control Act Amendments (1972), 17, 81, 84–7
Weather changes, 36, 53, 118–19
Wild and Scenic Rivers system, 102, 106–7, 112
Wilderness Act, 100, 104–5
Wilderness preservation, 19, 101–2, 104–6; in Alaska, 110–13
Wilderness Society, The, 165
Wildlife preservation, 19, 101–2, 109–10
Windmills, 44
Wood, recycling of, 77
World Directory of Environmental Organizations, 162
World Plan of Action (on population), 39–40
Worldwatch Institute, 166

XV nerve gas, 140

Zero Population Growth, 166
Zinc, 75, 91
Zoning, and land-use, 44

LIBRARY OF DAVIDSON COLLEGE

Books on regular loan may be checked out for **two weeks**. Books must be presented at the Circulation Desk in order to be renewed.

A fine is charged after date due.

Special books are subject to special regulations at the discretion of library staff.

OCT 1 1977			